KU-252-705

DK EYEWITNESS TOP 10 TRAVEL GUIDES

LOS ANGELES

CATHERINE GERBER

Left **Sunset Strip** Right **Huntington Gardens**

LONDON, NEW YORK,
MELBOURNE, MUNICH AND DELHI
www.dk.com

Reproduced by Colourscan, Singapore
Printed and bound in Italy by Graphicom

First published in Great Britain in 2004
by Dorling Kindersley Limited
80 Strand, London WC2R 0RL
A Penguin Company

**Reprinted with revisions 2006
Copyright 2004, 2006 ©
Dorling Kindersley Limited, London**

All rights reserved. No part of this publication may
be reproduced, stored in a retrieval system, or
transmitted in any form or by any means, electronic,
mechanical, photocopying, recording or otherwise,
without the prior written permission of the
copyright owner.

A CIP catalogue record is available from
the British Library.

UK ISBN 1405312343

Within each Top 10 list in this book, no
hierarchy of quality or popularity is
implied. All 10 are, in the editor's
opinion, of roughly equal merit.

Floors are referred to throughout in
accordance with American usage; ie the
"first floor" is at ground level.

Contents

Los Angeles Top 10

The information in this DK Eyewitness Top 10 Travel Guide is checked regularly.
Every effort has been made to ensure that this book is as up-to-date as possible at the time of
going to press. Some details, however, such as telephone numbers, opening hours, prices,
gallery hanging arrangements and travel information are liable to change. The publishers
cannot accept responsibility for any consequences arising from the use of this book, nor for
any material on third party websites, and cannot guarantee that any website address in this
book will be a suitable source of travel information. We value the views and suggestions of
our readers very highly. Please write to: Publisher, DK Eyewitness Travel Guides,
Dorling Kindersley, 80 Strand, London, Great Britain WC2R 0RL.

COVER: Front: **ALAMY IMAGES**: Stuart Dee main image; **DK IMAGES**: Neil Setchfield bl; clb.
Spine: **DK IMAGES**: Max Alexander. Back: **DK IMAGES**: Max Alexander tc; Neil Setchfield tl, tr.

Left **View of Downtown Los Angeles** Right *Homage to a Starry Night* **mural, Venice Beach**

Contents

Left **Redondo Beach** Right **Beverly Hills Hotel, Beverly Hills**

Key to abbreviations
Adm *admission charge* **Free** *no admission charge* **Dis. access** *disabled access*

3

LOS ANGELES
TOP 10

LOS ANGELES TOP 10

TOP 10 Los Angeles Highlights

The myth, the velocity, the edginess in creative and technological fields – this is Los Angeles, where the multicultural future that awaits the rest of the country is already a firm reality. In little more than 200 years, LA has grown from a dusty Spanish outpost into one of the world's largest and most complex cities offering top venues for everything from archaeology and the arts to food. The birthplace of Mickey Mouse and Hollywood, LA has shaped the imaginations of millions.

1 Sunset Strip
The heady mix of hip restaurants, nightclubs, and bars along the city's entertainment mile attracts legions of the young and the trendy *(see pp8–9).*

2 Historic Hollywood Boulevard
The boulevard that gave birth to the movie industry is still associated with the stars, even if the only ones around today are those embedded in the sidewalk *(see pp10–11).*

3 The Getty Center
One of the best bargains in town, this striking hilltop complex is a marvel of modern architecture and a mecca for fans of European art. Stunning views *(see pp12–15).*

4 Los Angeles County Museum of Art (LACMA)
One of the largest art museums in the US, LACMA offers a survey of artistic achievement in the world from prehistoric times to the present *(see pp16–19).*

Previous pages **View of LA from Griffith Observatory**

6 Huntington Library, Art Collections, & Botanical Gardens
One of LA's great cultural treasures invites visitors to experience its fine paintings, rare manuscripts, and gorgeous gardens *(see pp22–5)*.

5 El Pueblo de Los Angeles
This historic district preserves LA's oldest buildings, celebrating its Spanish-Mexican past with stores, eateries, and festivals *(see pp20–21)*.

7 Universal Studios Hollywood
A day at Universal involves high-tech thrill rides, live action shows, and special effects extravaganzas. The Studio Tour takes visitors to the backlot of this actual working movie studio *(see pp26–7)*.

8 Griffith Park
The largest city park in the nation offers a unique combination of rugged wilderness and such diversions as museums, a zoo, and an observatory. The landmark Hollywood Sign is located here as well *(see pp28–9)*.

9 Disneyland Resort
As timeless and ageless as Mickey Mouse himself, the original Disney park hasn't lost its magic nearly half a century after it first opened *(see pp30–35)*.

Catalina Island 10
Catalina Island is a quick and easy getaway whose considerable charms include crystal-clear waters, miles of undeveloped backcountry, and a sense of being far away from the bustle of big city LA *(see pp36–7)*.

TOP 10 Sunset Strip

Sunset Strip has been a haven of hedonism since Prohibition days. Wedged between Hollywood and Beverly Hills, this 1.7 miles (2.7 km) of the Sunset Boulevard is crammed with hot nightclubs, hip rock venues, and fashionable boutiques. During Hollywood's Glamour Age (1930–50), the stars trysted at the Chateau Marmont, partied at Trocadero, and talked shop at Schwab's Pharmacy. Today's hot spots rub shoulders with some historical landmarks.

1 Site of Schwab's Pharmacy

In the 1930s and 1940s, Schwab's Pharmacy was a hip hangout – Charlie Chaplin played pinball and James Dean sipped his coffee here. Torn down in 1988, the site is now occupied by a huge Virgin Megastore *(above)*.

The Strip by day

🍴 For fusion food at its finest, head to über-trendy Asia de Cuba inside the Mondrian Hotel *(see p147)*.

🕐 Gaining entry to the trendiest venues is easiest around 9pm and on weeknights.

Avoid the traffic on the Strip on Friday and Saturday nights.

• Map L3
• Along Sunset Blvd between Crescent Heights Blvd & Doheny Dr
• Site of Schwab's Pharmacy: 8024 Sunset Blvd
• Sunset Strip Tattoo: 7524 W Sunset Blvd
• Sunset Plaza: 8600 & 8700 Sunset Blvd
• Hyatt West Hollywood: 8401 Sunset Blvd
• Rainbow Bar & Grill: 9015 Sunset Blvd

Top 10 Sites

1. Site of Schwab's Pharmacy
2. Giant Billboards
3. Sunset Strip Tattoo
4. Chateau Marmont
5. The Argyle hotel
6. Sunset Plaza
7. Viper Room
8. Whisky a Go-Go
9. Hyatt West Hollywood
10. Rainbow Bar & Grill

2 Giant Billboards

A testimony to the Strip's unabashed commercialism, these mega-sized billboards promote movies, records, products, and individual stars, which is why they're also called "vanity boards" *(above)*.

3 Sunset Strip Tattoo

Julia Roberts got a Japanese symbol and Nicolas Cage a stingray at this tattoo studio to the stars that has also inked Ben Affleck and Pamela Anderson.

Sunset Strip by night

4 Chateau Marmont

Modeled on a French palace, this 1927 hotel *(below & p146)* has hosted celebrities such as Humphrey Bogart and Mick Jagger. Howard Hughes ogled at girls by the pool, and an overdosed John Belushi made his final dramatic exit in 1982.

The Argyle hotel
This Art Deco gem *(above & p146)* began life as the Sunset Tower in 1931 and has been the home of yesteryear stars. John Wayne allegedly kept a cow in the penthouse. Its bar is a hot address today.

Sunset Plaza
This two-block commercial stretch is lined with designer shops and Euro-style restaurants teeming with a hip crowd. Its appeal with celebrities such as Nicole Kidman and Cindy Crawford make it prime territory for star-searching *(below)*.

Viper Room
Actor River Phoenix died outside this Johnny Depp-owned club in 1993 after a drug cocktail. Few remember its earlier incarnation as the Melody Room, a favorite with Bugsy Siegel and his mobster pals *(see p106)*.

Whisky a Go-Go
A Strip fixture since 1963, the Whisky gave the world go-go dancing and the Doors, its house band in 1966. Other legends such as Jimi Hendrix and Janis Joplin also played here regularly. Today, new bands still get launched on occasion *(see p106)*.

Hyatt West Hollywood
Nicknamed the "Riot Hyatt," this hotel tower is part of rock'n'roll history as party central for British bands in the 1960s and 1970s. Led Zeppelin cruised down the halls on motorcycles and Keith Richards mooned his fans.

Rainbow Bar & Grill
This rock'n'roll *boîte* fills with long-haired rockers and their hangers-on every night. When it was still the Villa Nova restaurant, Marilyn Monroe met Joe DiMaggio on a blind date, and John Belushi ate his final meal before overdosing on drugs.

Sunset Boulevard

Sunset Strip takes up only a small portion of the 25-mile (40-km) Sunset Boulevard. Following the path of an old Indian Trail, this major cross-town artery is a microcosm of the cultural, ethnic, and social cauldron that is LA. Starting at El Pueblo in downtown, it travels west through different neighborhoods such as Silver Lake, Los Feliz, Hollywood, Beverly Hills, Bel Air, and Pacific Palisades before spilling into the Pacific Ocean. Sunset Boulevard has played starring roles in the TV series *77 Sunset Strip* and the movie *Sunset Boulevard*.

Historic Hollywood Boulevard

Hollywood Boulevard, home of the Walk of Fame, has always been synonymous with the glamour of moviemaking, especially during its heydays in the 1920s and 1930s. But like an aging diva, it eventually fell out of favor, teeming with runaways, drug addicts, and prostitutes. Now the heart of Tinseltown is finally cleaning up its act – the old movie palaces have received facelifts, the mega-entertainment complex of Hollywood and Highland is a major draw, and even "Oscar" has found a permanent home here.

Hand- & Footprints in Mann's Chinese Theatre

🍴 For the yummiest cakes, head for Café Mozart, inside the Hollywood and Highland complex.

⭐ Red signs along the boulevard indicate places the stars used to hang out in.

The visitors center at the Hollywood and Highland is open 10am–10pm Mon–Sat, 10am–7pm Sun.

• Map P2
• *Stretches from La Brea Blvd to Vine St*
• *Walk of Fame: Hollywood Blvd between Gower St & La Brea Ave, and Vine St between Yucca Ave & Sunset Blvd*
• *Hollywood Entertainment Museum: 7021 Hollywood Blvd*
• *Hollywood & Highland: 6801 Hollywood Blvd*
• *Frederick's of Hollywood Lingerie Museum: 6608 Hollywood Blvd*
• *Capitol Records Tower: 1750 N Vine St*

Top 10 Features

1. Walk of Fame
2. Hollywood Entertainment Museum
3. Hollywood Roosevelt Hotel
4. Mann's Chinese Theatre
5. El Capitan Theatre
6. Hollywood & Highland
7. The Egyptian Theatre
8. Frederick's of Hollywood Lingerie Museum
9. Capitol Records Tower
10. Pantages Theatre

1 Walk of Fame
Elvis, Lassie, and over 2,000 other celebs have been immortalized with a marble-encased brass star in the sidewalk *(above)*. Only those working in the movies, TV, radio, recording, or theater are eligible.

2 Hollywood Entertainment Museum
This museum offers a behind-the-scenes look at the entertainment industry. Highlights include a scale model of 1940s Hollywood, and original sets from blockbusters such as *Star Trek* and the *X-Files*.

3 Hollywood Roosevelt Hotel
Douglas Fairbanks Sr. presided over the inaugural Academy Awards here *(below & p146)* in 1929 and Marilyn Monroe shot her first commercial by the pool, later adorned with blue squiggles by the artist David Hockney.

4 Mann's Chinese Theatre

The world's most famous movie theater *(below & p56)* opened in 1927 with a screening of Cecil B. De Mille's *King of Kings*. About 200 stars have left their hand- and foot-prints here, not to mention Betty Grable's famous legs.

7 The Egyptian Theatre

Now owned by the American Cinematheque, a nonprofit film organization, this 1922 theater is the birthplace of the "Hollywood premiere" *(see p56)*.

9 Capitol Records Tower

The world's first circular office building resembles a stack of records topped by a stylus that blinks out "Hollywood" in Morse code. It opened in 1956 as the head-quarters of the music giant, Capitol Records.

10 Pantages Theatre

The grande dame of Tinseltown theaters sparkles once again in restored Art Deco glory. The lobby leads to the magnificent auditorium with its three-dimensional ceiling. It now hosts blockbuster Broadway shows *(see p55)*.

5 El Capitan Theatre

The strikingly ornate 1926 El Capitan *(above & p56)* was Hollywood's first live theater and began screening films in 1941. Today, it functions as a Disney first-run movie theater.

6 Hollywood & Highland

This cornerstone of Hollywood revitalization combines shops, restaurants, night clubs, movie theaters, a hotel, and the 3,600-seat Kodak Theatre, home of the Oscars.

8 Frederick's of Hollywood Lingerie Museum

Famous for its vast assortment of lingerie, Frederick's *(below)* does double duty as a hall of fame for celebrity underwear. The collection includes bustiers worn by Marilyn and Madonna, and Cher's bras.

A Star for the Stars

A star on the Walk of Fame requires the prior approval of a screening committee appointed by the Hollywood Chamber of Commerce. Of the 200 applications received every year, only 10 percent get the nod – and the privilege to pay the $15,000 for installation and mainte-nance. Studios, and sometimes, fan clubs, usually foot the bill. Induction ceremonies are held once or twice a month and are open to the public. Check out www.hollywoodcoc.org for who's up next.

⑩ The Getty Center

An exquisite art collection, superb architecture, and lovely gardens combine with a hilltop location to create one of LA's finest cultural destinations. Designed by Richard Meier, the Getty Center opened in December 1997 after 14 years of planning and construction. It unites the entities of the Getty Trust created by oil tycoon John P. Getty (1892–1976), including research and conservation institutes. At its core, however, is the museum with exquisite European art from Roman sculpture to Impressionist paintings.

Steps leading to the Getty Museum

🍴 Bring your own picnic to enjoy along with the views in the gardens or courtyard, or pick up a light meal at a kiosk or the self-service café. For great gourmet meals, book a table at The Restaurant.

🧒 Unlike most art museums, the Getty welcomes kids with special children-oriented audioguides and a staffed Family Room filled with games and various hands-on activities.

Take advantage of the free architecture and garden tours that the Getty offers through the day.

- Map C2
- 1200 Getty Center Dr, Brentwood
- 310-440-7300
- Open 10am–6pm Tue–Thu & Sun, 10am–9pm Fri & Sat
- Free, parking $5
- www.getty.edu

Top 10 Artworks

1. Irises
2. Young Italian Woman
3. Wheatstacks, Snow Effect, Morning
4. Landsdowne Herakles
5. The Abduction of Europa
6. Venus & Adonis
7. Christ's Entry into Brussels in 1889
8. La Promenade
9. Cabinet on Stand
10. The Adoration of the Magi

1 Irises
Van Gogh (1853–90) painted this exquisite work *(right)* in the last year of his life in a mental asylum. The intense color and energetic composition borrow from Gauguin and Japanese printmaker Hokusai.

2 Young Italian Woman
Often called the "Father of Modern Art," Cézanne's (1839–1906) emotionally charged painting of a melancholy young woman shows off his great versatility and technical prowess.

3 Wheatstacks, Snow Effect, Morning
This is one of 30 works which Claude Monet (1840–1926) painted between 1890 and 1891. Set against a soft sky and faintly visible houses, the wheatstacks are a solid, imposing presence *(right)*.

4 Landsdowne Herakles
This Roman copy of a Greek original dates from about AD 125 and was excavated from the villa of Emperor Hadrian. It depicts the Greek hero Herakles with his club, carrying the skin of the lion he has killed in his right hand.

On Friday nights the Getty features poets, performers, and journalists in the Harold M. Williams Auditorium

6 Venus & Adonis

Mythology was a favorite subject of Titian (c.1485–1576). This painting *(left)* shows a beseeching Venus trying to prevent Adonis from leaving for the hunt that leads to his death.

9 Cabinet on Stand

This cabinet *(above)* celebrates the triumphs of the French king, Louis XIV. Attributed to André-Charles Boulle (1642–1732), pewter and tortoiseshell are some of the materials used.

10 The Adoration of the Magi

In this Renaissance masterpiece, Andrea Mantegna (c.1431–1506) emulates the compact composition of ancient Roman reliefs to achieve a sense of intimacy between subjects. The three kings represent Europe, Asia, and Africa.

5 The Abduction of Europa

Rembrandt (1606–69) found great inspiration in Ovid's *Metamorphoses*. This work *(below)* captures a dramatic moment: Jupiter, disguised as a white bull, spirits away the princess Europa across the oceans.

7 Christ's Entry into Brussels in 1889

Belgian James Ensor's (1860–1949) painting is one of the most controversial works of the 19th century. The grotesque scene reflects the artist's uneasiness with contemporary society.

8 La Promenade

An homage to his favorite artists such as Watteau and Courbet, this early Impressionist painting by Renoir (1841–1919) shows a young couple coyly heading for the woods.

Museum Guide

The tall, airy entrance hall of the Getty opens into a central courtyard. From here radiate five two-story pavilions, four of which present works in chronological order from the museum's permanent collection. The fifth is dedicated to temporary exhibitions. The skylit upper floors feature paintings, while the lower ones display sculpture, illuminated manuscripts, and other treasures. CD-ROM audioguides for self-guided tours are available to rent. The central garden hugs a natural ravine below.

Left **Electric Tram** Center **Panoramic Views** Right **Central Garden**

Top 10 Features of the Getty

1 Electric Tram
The Getty experience kicks off with a smooth five-minute ride up the hill from the entrance gate to the Arrival Plaza in a driver-less, computer-operated tram.

2 Panoramic Views
On clear days, the views from Getty's hilltop perch are spectacular, especially around sunset. Take in the vastness of LA's labyrinthine streets, the Santa Monica Mountains, and the Pacific Ocean.

3 Central Garden
These beautiful, constantly changing gardens were designed by visual artist Robert Irwin (b.1928). Wander along tree-lined paths and across a gentle stream to a reflecting pool with floating azaleas and ringed by beautiful specialty gardens.

4 Art Information Rooms
Located in each of the main pavilions, these education centers contain displays, books, and multimedia computer stations for those seeking in-depth information on a particular artist, period, or work.

5 Decorative Arts
The Getty's famous collection of French decorative art and furniture from the 17th and 18th centuries is displayed in a series of period rooms. The paneled Régence salon from 1710 is a must-see.

6 Illuminated Manuscripts
Shown on a rotating basis, the Getty's collection of illuminated manuscripts covers the entire Middle Ages and Renaissance. The *Stammheim Missal* (1120) from Germany is among the most prized.

7 Drawings
Highlights of this collection, dating from the 14th to the 19th centuries, include Albrecht Dürer's exquisite *The Stag Beetle* (1505) and Leonardo da Vinci's *Studies for the Christ Child with Lamb* (c.1503–06).

8 Photography
Known for its images from the early 1840s, this department's collection concentrates on work by European and American artists. Man Ray's *Tears* is among the most famous pieces.

9 European Art
The museum's collection of European paintings is small but choice. Paintings from the Italian Renaissance and Baroque periods, as well as French Impressionism, are particularly well represented.

10 Antiquities
Sculpture and vases form the heart of the antiquities collection. In 2005, it will move into the restored Getty Villa in Malibu, which is modeled on a 1st-century Roman country house.

Top 10 Building Statistics

1. Campus size: 110 acres
2. Campus altitude: 881 ft (264 m)
3. Cost: $1 billion
4. Cubic yards (of earth) moved: 1.5 million
5. Travertine used: 16,000 tons
6. Weight of each travertine block: 280 pounds (126 kg)
7. Enameled aluminum panels: 40,000
8. Exterior glass: 164,650 sq ft (14,820 sq m)
9. Number of doors: 3,200
10. Length of tram ride: 0.7 miles (1.2 km)

The Architecture

Detail of façade

Roosting on its hilltop site on the edge of the Santa Monica Mountains, the Getty Center is an imposing presence, far removed from city noise and bustle. An amazing feat of architecture and engineering, it was designed by New York-based Modernist Richard Meier (b.1930), an internationally acclaimed architect who also drafted the Museum of Television and Radio in Beverly Hills (see p111). For the Getty, Meier arranged the main buildings along two natural ridges connected by creative landscaping. Curvilinear elements, such as in the Museum Entrance Hall, combine with angular structures to create an effect of fluidity and openness. This is further enhanced by the use of travertine, a honey-colored stone quarried in Italy, which covers most buildings. Many of the stones bear fossilized leaves and feathers.

A Modern "Acropolis"

Seen from above, the Getty Center looks like a bunker atop a hill. But once you're within, walking beneath curvilinear balconies, across acres of rich gleaming stone, and through wondrous green gardens, you begin to see the Getty as a sort of modern – and thoroughly American – "Acropolis": classic and timeless.

The Getty's distinctive curvilinear architecture

TOP10 Los Angeles County Museum of Art (LACMA)

The largest encyclopedic art museum in the western US, LACMA was founded in 1910 and moved to its present Miracle Mile home in 1965. It now consists of six buildings, including the remarkable Pavilion for Japanese Art and the LACMA West annex. The museum's treasure trove includes paintings by Dürer, Monet, and Picasso; American and Latin American art; and work from around the Middle East and Asia. Special exhibits and a lively schedule of concerts, lectures, and film screenings make LACMA a community destination.

Ceci n'est pas une pipe by Rene Magritte, 1928

⊙ Good places to rest your feet are the Plaza Café, which serves light meals and refreshments, and the more formal Pentimento with a full menu and bar.

♫ Free jazz concerts draw a sizable crowd on Friday nights (5:30–8:30pm) from April to December. The free Sunday chamber music series is also quite popular.

• Map N6
• 5905 Wilshire Blvd, Midtown
• 323-857-6000
• Open noon–8pm Mon, Tue, & Thu, noon–9pm Fri, 11am–8pm Sat–Sun
• Adm $9/$5/free for adult/senior/under 17s, free second Tue of the month, extra charge for special exhibits
• www.lacma.org

Top 10 Collections

1. American Art
2. Ancient & Islamic Art
3. South & Southeast Asian Art
4. Chinese & Korean Art
5. Japanese Art
6. Modern & Contemporary Art
7. Latin American Art
8. European Painting & Sculpture
9. Photography, Prints, & Drawings
10. Decorative Arts

Ahmanson Building

1 American Art
This collection offers a survey of American art from the 1700s to the 1940s. Among the highlights are works by late 19th-century figurative artists such as Winslow Homer. Other works include paintings by George Bellows and Mary Cassatt, specifically *Mother About to Wash her Sleepy Child (above)*.

2 Ancient & Islamic Art
Egyptian tomb reliefs, glass from ancient Greece, bronzes from Syria, and ceramics from Mexico are prized items from ancient cultures. Even more renowned is the Islamic collection.

3 South & Southeast Asian Art
This collection is one of the finest, with stone sculpture, watercolors, drawings, ritual art, and coins. Among the highlights are Indian art and sculpture from some Southeast Asian countries.

→ *Every Tuesday at 1pm, the museum presents a classic film in the Bing Theater*

Chinese & Korean Art
Paintings, metalwork, and Buddhist art from the third century BC to the 20th century are part of this collection - The recreated Ming-period scholar's studio is a standout.

5 Japanese Art
The Pavilion for Japanese Art is the only building outside Japan solely devoted to its art. It houses superb Edo-period paintings and exquisite porcelain.

6 Modern & Contemporary Art
LACMA has a growing collection of art from 1900 to the present in media ranging from painting to video installations. Kandinsky, Matisse, Picasso, Mark Rothko, and David Hockney are among those represented.

8 European Painting & Sculpture
An exquisite collection that encompasses works by Flemish and Dutch masters and French Impressionists, including Monet's *In the Woods at Giverny* (above).

9 Photography, Prints, & Drawings
Work by photographers such as Alfred Stieglitz and Edward Weston and prints and drawings by Dürer, Toulouse-Lautrec, and others are shown in rotating exhibitions.

10 Decorative Arts
This collection has a wide range of European and American furniture, metalwork, and glass from the Middle Ages to today. The Palevsky Arts and Crafts collection is very comprehensive.

Hammer Building

Pavilion for Japanese Art

Bing Center

Anderson Building

Key
■ Lower Level
■ Plaza Level
■ Second Level
■ Third Level

7 Latin American Art
A new gallery in LACMA West displays major works by a veritable who's who in Latin American art, including Frida Kahlo and muralists such as Diego Rivera, whose iconic *Flower Day* (left) is displayed.

Gallery Guide
LACMA's permanent collection is displayed in five buildings. American and European art are on the first and second floors of the Ahmanson Building, which also presents Islamic and Asian art. The Hammer Building houses 19th-century European art as well as changing photography, prints, and drawing exhibitions. Next door is the Pavilion for Japanese Art and across the courtyard the Anderson Building with modern and contemporary art. LACMA West contains the Latin American galleries.

LACMA's Art Rental & Sales Gallery is located on the lower level of the Bing Center

Left **LACMA** Center *Untitled Improvisation III* Right *Magdalen with the Smoking Flame*

Top 10 LACMA Masterpieces

1 Portrait of Mrs Edward L. Davis & Her Son, Livingston Davis
John Singer Sargent (1856–1925) was a gifted and prolific East Coast society portrait painter. This 1890 work blends loose brushwork (the boy) with stark realism (the woman's head).

2 Standing Warrior
Standing about 3-ft (1-m) tall, this figure of a king or warrior is the largest known effigy from western Mexico and was fired in one piece. It dates from between 100 BC and AD 300.

3 Eagle-headed Deity
Ancient Syrian palaces were often decorated with intricately carved stone slabs. This one depicts a deity in the process of fertilizing a tree by scattering pollen from a pail.

4 Shiva as the Lord of Dance
This exquisite sculpture from the tenth century portrays the Hindu god Shiva as the source of cosmic dance, which defines the universe as a cycle of creation, preservation, and destruction.

5 Untitled Improvisation III
A pioneer of pure abstract painting, Russian-born Wassily Kandinsky (1866–1944) imbued his canvasses with spirituality expressed through shapes and bold colors, as in this 1914 work.

6 Flower Day
Mexican artist Diego Rivera (1886–1957) is best known for his murals and as Frida Kahlo's husband, but the famous *Flower Day* (1925) shows off his talent as a Cubist-influenced painter.

7 Magdalen with the Smoking Flame
French Baroque artist Georges de la Tour (1593–1652) employs deep contrasts between light and shadow to depict his subject with great intimacy and realism.

"Standing Warrior"

8 Majolica Dish
The Italian town of Urbino was once a major center of ceramics production. This elaborate 1531 plate by Francesco Xanto Avelli da Rovigo features a scene from the epic *Orlando Furioso*.

9 Mulholland Drive
LA-based British artist David Hockney created many panoramic paintings such as this brightly colored and dynamically composed one. This 1980 work shows the famous LA road linking the artist's house and studio.

10 Chest of Drawers
Gold and silver leaf embellish a surface composed of dozens of coats of lacquer on this masterful chest showing famous scenes around Lake Biwa. It was made by Yamamoto Shunsho in 18th-century Kyoto.

Top 10 of Art Deco on the Miracle Mile

1. May Co. Department Store (now LACMA West), 1940: Wilshire at Fairfax Ave
2. El Rey Theater (1928): 5515 Wilshire Blvd
3. Desmonds Department Store Building (1929): 5514 Wilshire Blvd
4. Commercial Building (1927): 5464 Wilshire Blvd
5. Roman's Food Mart (1935): 5413 Wilshire Blvd
6. Chandler's Shoe Store (1938): Wilshire at Cloverdale Ave
7. Dominguez-Wilshire Blvd (1930): 5410 Wilshire Blvd
8. The Dark Room (1938): 5370 Wilshire Blvd
9. Wilson Building (1930): 5217-5231 Wilshire Blvd
10. Security Pacific Bank Building (1929): 5209 Wilshire Blvd

Museum Row
With its four museums, including LACMA, the western end of Miracle Mile is also known as "Museum Row."

The Miracle Mile sign

The Miracle Mile

LACMA sits on a particularly interesting and historic stretch of Wilshire Boulevard. The so-called "Miracle Mile" was LA's first shopping district outside of downtown and the first ever designed with easy access for the motorized shopper. The man behind this vision was developer A.W. Ross who, in 1921, bought 18 acres of land between La Brea Boulevard and Fairfax Avenue with the lofty goal of turning it into a "Fifth Avenue of the West." His plan succeeded wildly, as department stores and upscale retail establishments quickly moved in, but it also marked the beginning of LA's decentralization. By the 1960s, however, a new innovation – the shopping mall – spelled the end of the "miracle." Although a shadow of its former self, the Miracle Mile has been revitalized to some extent with the stylish Conga Room (see p60) and galleries attracting their share of the hip lot. A few of the Art Deco buildings have survived and are now on the National Register of Historic Places.

May Company building (now LACMA West)

The Los Angeles Art Deco Society (310-659-3326) offers walking tours of the Miracle Mile

El Pueblo de Los Angeles

This historic district protects LA's oldest structures, all built between 1818 and 1926. Close to the site where 44 Mexican men, women, and children established El Pueblo de Los Angeles in the name of the Spanish crown in 1781, it also reflects the heritage of other ethnic groups that arrived later, including the Chinese, Italians, and French. As LA grew into a metropolis, businesses relocated to newer neighborhoods and the area plunged into deep decline. Now beautifully restored, three of its 27 structures contain museums.

Olvera Street marketplace

⊙ Olvera Street is a great place for an authentic Mexican meal. Try the ever-popular Casa Golondrina or the more casual La Luz del Dia.

✪ Volunteer docents offer free guided tours of El Pueblo at 10am, 11am, and noon Tuesday to Saturday. Check in next to the firehouse. The visitor center offers self-guided tour pamphlets.

• Map W4
• El Pueblo Visitor Center: Sepulveda House, Olvera Street, 213-628-1274, Open 10am–3pm Mon–Sat, www.olvera-street.com
• Olvera Street market: Open 10am–7pm daily (some shops may open earlier and close later)
• Avila Adobe: Open 9am–3pm daily, free
• Old Plaza Firehouse: Open 10am–3pm Tue–Sun, free

Top 10 Sights

1. Olvera Street
2. América Tropical
3. Sepulveda House
4. Avila Adobe
5. Blessing of the Animals
6. Old Plaza Church
7. Old Plaza
8. Old Plaza Firehouse
9. Pico House
10. Chinese American Museum

1 Olvera Street

Named after LA's first county judge, this bustling, brick-paved lane has been a Mexican marketplace since 1930. Wander past colorful carts overflowing with folk art and curios or try some tasty tacos and *tortas*.

2 América Tropical

El Pueblo is home to a rare mural by Mexican artist David Alfaro Siqueiros. Painted in 1932, this controversial work is a visceral allegory about the exploitation of Mexican workers.

3 Sepulveda House

Eloisa Sepulveda built this lovely Victorian house *(above)* in 1887 as her home, a hotel, and stores. Today, it contains El Pueblo's visitor center.

4 Avila Adobe

LA's oldest surviving house *(below)* was built by mayor Don Francisco Avila in 1818 and went through several incarnations as a military headquarters and boarding house. The restored rooms offer a glimpse of 1840s life.

 The information booth at 130 Paseo de la Plaza offers free guided walking tours

7 Old Plaza

Music, dancing, and merriment fills the Old Plaza *(left)* during lively fiestas. Sculptures of King Carlos III of Spain and Felipe de Neve, and a plaque listing the names of El Pueblo's original settlers, honor LA's founders.

9 Pico House

Pio Pico, the last Mexican governor of California, built this grand Italianate edifice *(above)* in 1870. It was LA's first three-story structure and once housed a hotel.

10 Chinese American Museum

The Chinese first settled in and around El Pueblo in the late 19th century. A new museum (to open in 2004) in the 1890s Garnier Building traces the community's history.

5 Blessing of the Animals

Leo Polti's endearing 1978 mural *(above)* shows the centuries-old Mexican tradition of thanking animals – canaries to cows – for the joy and service they provide humans. Celebrations take place in the Old Plaza each year.

6 Old Plaza Church

Worshipers have gathered in LA's oldest church since 1822. The original was rebuilt in 1861 and several alterations have taken place since then. Features include the painted ceiling and the main altar framed in gold leaf *(right)*.

8 Old Plaza Firehouse

This two-story brick building is a must-see. Firehouse No.1 with its all-volunteer crew and horse-drawn equipment remained operational until 1897. Check out a small exhibit of fire fighting memorabilia.

The Mother of Olvera Street

Had it not been for Christine Sterling (1881–1963), an LA socialite turned civic activist, the El Pueblo de Los Angeles area would still remain a railway station. Dismayed by the seediness of LA's oldest neighborhood, Sterling launched her 1926 campaign to save it. Her dedication earned her the backing of *LA Times* publisher Harry Chandler and others. In April 1930, Olvera Street was reincarnated as a bustling Mexican market. The Avila Adobe contains an exhibit on Sterling's triumph.

TOP 10 Huntington Library, Art Collections, & Botanical Gardens

The Huntington is one of those rare places that manages to please the eye, stimulate the mind, and nourish the soul all at the same time. The former estate of railroad and real estate baron Henry E. Huntington (1850–1927), it consists of a trio of treasures: the art collections include fine examples of British, French, and American art; the Huntington Library has about four million rare manuscripts and books, including a Gutenberg Bible; and the Botanical Gardens are a fantastic feast of flora in a pleasing parklike setting.

Huntington Library

🍴 Picnicking, alas, is not permitted, but a self-service restaurant serves light meals and refreshments. Better yet, make reservations (626-683-8131) for English tea served in the Rose Garden Room, a time-honored Huntington tradition.

🌿 Amazing plants from the Huntington nursery are available for purchase during the Garden Talk and Sale event held every second Thursday of the month.

- Map F2
- 1151 Oxford Rd, San Marino near Pasadena
- 626-405-2100
- Open noon–4:30pm Tue–Fri, 10:30am–4:30pm Sat–Sun, 10:30am–4:30pm daily in summer
- Adm $15/$12/$10/$6/free for adult/senior/student 12–18/child 5–11/under 5s, free 1st Thu of month

Top 10 Features

1. Japanese Garden
2. Desert Garden
3. Chaucer's "The Canterbury Tales"
4. Gutenberg Bible
5. Rose Garden
6. Bonsai Court
7. North Vista
8. Greene & Greene Exhibit
9. Boone Gallery
10. Camellia Garden

1 Japanese Garden
A place for strolling and quiet contemplation, Huntington's Japanese Garden *(right)* is among America's oldest of its kind. Its canyon setting is accented by a shimmering pond filled with *koi* fish and lovely water lilies.

2 Desert Garden
This exotic garden *(below)* with its clusters of whimsical cacti and flowering succulents, has an otherworldly feel. One of the world's finest, it's a study of the ways in which desert plants adapt to survive in harsh conditions.

3 Chaucer's "The Canterbury Tales"
This rare 1410 manuscript of English poet Geoffrey Chaucer's most famous work is complete, in marvellous condition, and filled with luminous illustrations. It's perhaps better known as the "Ellesmere Manuscript," after its former owner, the Earl of Ellesmere.

For useful information on the Huntington log on to www.huntington.org

4 Gutenberg Bible

The Huntington Library's star exhibit, this 1455 Bible *(left)* is one of only 12 surviving copies printed on vellum (calf or sheep skin) by Johannes Gutenberg of Mainz, Germany, the inventor of movable type. The colorful chapter headings and decorations were added by hand.

8 Greene & Greene Exhibit

Charles and Henry Greene, known for their wooden houses and fine furnishings, were the first to practice the early 20th-century Craftsman style *(see p91)*.

9 Boone Gallery

The newest gallery space at the Huntington, the Boone began life in 1911 as a garage. With columns that echo the Neo-Classical style of the mansion, it is used for temporary exhibitions.

10 Camellia Garden

Camellias reached the Western world in the 18th century. With about 1,200 varieties (in bloom from January to March), this garden has one of the finest collections.

6 Bonsai Court

The art of grooming and training trees into fully mature but dwarf-sized versions originated in ancient China and Japan. This small but exquisite collection includes specimens of California juniper, gingko, and Japanese black pine.

5 Rose Garden

This romantic garden *(above)* brings you nearly 1,800 rose varieties, some of them with a pedigree going back to ancient Greece. These noble blossoms may be enjoyed from March right through December, May is the peak month.

7 North Vista

The palms and stone statues lining the central lawn of this Baroque garden reminds one of European palaces. It connects the Huntington Gallery with a dolphin-studded Italian fountain against a San Gabriel mountain backdrop.

A Short Guide

Access the Huntington from either Orlando Road or Oxford Road. Both lead to a large parking lot and from there to the entrance pavilion, where you can pick up a free map. An excellent museum store stocks art books and quality gifts. While you can "do" the Huntington in an hour or two, it's really the kind of place that is meant to be savored. Come early and spend the day.

Left **Huntington Art Gallery** Center *Chimborazo* Right *The Long Leg*

Top 10 Huntington Artworks

1 Blue Boy
Thomas Gainsborough (1727–88) was the most sought-after portrait painter of British high society. This famous 1770 painting shows Jonathan Buttall, a friend of the artist, in 16th-century costume.

2 Pinkie
Thomas Lawrence (1769–1830) painted Sarah Barrett Moulton, nicknamed "Pinkie," aged 11, in a refreshingly direct and lively manner. She died shortly after the completion of this painting, probably of consumption.

3 View on the Stour near Dedham
Romantic landscape painter John Constable (1776–1837) adopted a lyrical approach to depicting nature. His emphasis on sky, light, and other intangible qualities greatly influenced other artists, including the Impressionists.

4 Madonna & Child
A master of early Flemish painting, Rogier van der Weyden (1400–64) infused his works with emotional intensity, evident here in the Virgin's face and hands.

Madonna and Child by Rogier van der Weyden (1400–64)

5 The Grand Canal, Venice
This 1837 painting is a fine example of the translucency typical of the works of J.M.W. Turner (1775–1851). The tiny person in the lower right corner is Shylock from the play *The Merchant of Venice*.

6 The Western Brothers
John Singleton Copley (1738–1815) was born in Colonial Boston and moved to England just before 1776. This 1783 double portrait is characterized by flowing strokes and strong expressions on the faces of the young men.

7 Chimborazo
A trip to Ecuador inspired this painting by 19th-century American landscape artist, Frederic Church (1826–1900). Church took creative license when compressing the mountains, desert, and jungle into a single image.

8 Breakfast in Bed
Pennsylvania-born Mary Cassatt (1844–1926) moved to Paris in 1873 where she befriended Degas and fell under the spell of Impressionism. The subject of mother and child was a favorite.

The Huntingdon Art Gallery is currently undergoing renovations

9 The Long Leg

The solitude and anonymity of human existence is a recurring theme in the paintings of Edward Hopper (1882–1967), a leading 20th-century American Realist. Here, these sentiments of loneliness are expressed in a famous sailing scene.

10 The Robinson Dining Room

This recreated dining room exemplifies the innovative genius of the brothers Charles and Henry Greene. Designed between 1905 and 1907, it contains original furniture and an amazing chandelier.

Huntington Art Gallery First Floor Plan

Huntington Library First Floor Plan

Virginia Steele Scott Gallery of American Art First Floor Plan

Top 10 Big Red Cars Facts & Stats

1. Covered four counties
2. Linked 50 communities
3. First ride: 1901
4. Last ride: 1961
5. Track: 1,150 miles (1,850 km)
6. Fleet: 900 cars at peak
7. Passengers: 109 million in 1944 (peak year)
8. Fare: a penny a mile
9. Top speed: 40–50 mph (60–80 km/h)
10. Car length: 50 ft (15 m)

Henry Huntington's Big Red Cars

Henry E. Huntington made his vast fortune by marrying real estate speculation with public transportation. The largest landowner in Southern California, he established the Pacific Electric Railway in 1901, primarily to get people out to the far-flung new suburbs he was developing. Soon Huntington's fleet of interurban red trolleys – dubbed the "Big Red Cars" – became the world's largest electric-transit system, linking communities throughout Southern California. By the time he sold most of his holdings to the Southern Pacific Railroad in 1910, the population of LA had tripled to around 310,000. "The last trolley" made its farewell voyage in 1961.

Pacific Electric Engine on display in Travel Town, Griffith Park

 A new wing was added to the Virginia Steele Scott Gallery of American Art in May 2005

🔟 Universal Studios® Hollywood

The world's largest movie and television studio sprang from the imagination of cinema pioneer Carl Laemmle. In 1915 he bought a former chicken ranch, brought in cameras, lights, and actors and started making silent films. The theme park began taking shape in 1964. Today, Universal Studios Hollywood gets more visitors (about five million a year) than any other attraction in LA County. Among the studio's greatest film hits are Jurassic Park (1993) and Shrek (2001).

Shrek 4-D
4 The award-winning hit *Shrek* comes to life in this state-of-the-art attraction featuring ground-breaking *OgreVision* animation and sensory immersion. Voice-overs include comic talents Eddie Murphy, Mike Myers and Cameron Diaz.

The Universal Studios Hollywood sign

🍴 Dining inside the park is limited to snack bars and self-service restaurants. For a sit-down meal, get your hand stamped for re-entry and head to CityWalk's many superb restaurants.

🎫 Beat the crowds with the Front-of-the-Line Ticket or the guided VIP Experience, which includes an expanded Studio Tour (tours also run daily in Spanish). Prices vary.

- Map D2
- 100 Universal City Plaza, Universal City
- 800-Universal
- Seasonal hours vary. Call for details.
- Adm $49.75/$39.75/ free for adult/child under 4 ft (1.2 m) tall/under 3s, discounted tickets available online
- Print-at-home ticketing is available at www.universalstudios hollywood.com

Top 10 Features
1. Studio Tour
2. Revenge of The Mummy – The Ride
3. Back to the Future
4. Shrek 4-D
5. Animal Planet Live!
6. Jurassic Park – The Ride
7. Terminator 2: 3D
8. Water World
9. CityWalk
10. Meeting the "Stars"

Studio Tour
1 For a look at movie-making, this 45-minute narrated tram tour of the actual working studio is a must. Cruise past 35 soundstages to the vast backlot with its fabled outdoor sets *(right)*.

Revenge of The Mummy – The Ride
2 The park's first ever roller coaster is a psychological thrill ride that will bring you face to face with the fear of darkness, of insects, of speed, and of heights.

Back to the Future
3 Christopher Lloyd as "Doc Brown" enlists guests as time-travel volunteers in this motion simulator adventure. Hop into his DeLorean for a wild ride that takes you through volcanoes *(right)*.

Animal Planet Live!
5 A psychic bull terrier, an obstreperous orangutan, and a thieving parakeet are just some of the endearing animal stars performing hilarious tricks during this 10-minute show. The kids will absolutely love this!

➡️ **Note:** *The simulated earthquakes and floods in the tram tour may be rather frightening for very young children*

Lower Lot | Escalator Down to Lower Lot

2

6

3

5

1

Upper Lot | Blast Zone

4

7 | The Blues Brothers

Universal Amphitheatre

8

Entrance

9 Universal Citywalk

6 Jurassic Park – The Ride

A gentle rafting trip through a lush primordial park inhabited by cloned dinosaurs turns into a nightmare as guests come face to face with a voracious T-Rex *(above)*. The only escape is an 84-ft (25-m) plunge that leaves everyone drenched.

9 CityWalk

A lively carnival atmosphere reigns along this studio-adjacent promenade with its mix of restaurants, shops, and entertainment venues. The best time to visit is after sunset when huge neon signs turn CityWalk into a miniature Las Vegas Strip.

10 Meeting the "Stars"

Chances of running into a real celebrity are slim, but don't fret – there'll be plenty of photo ops with actors dressed as classic silver screen stars such as Charlie Chaplin or even some favorite cartoon characters.

Studio Guide

Universal Studios is divided into upper and lower sections linked by a multi-segmented escalator, the world's second longest. All visitors receive an orientation map that also lists that day's show times. Note that it's about a 10-minute stroll along CityWalk from the parking lot to the box office. The park is least busy midweek in the off-season (October to April). In summer, arrive before doors open and race to the most popular attractions first.

8 Water World

For the best stunts, catch this show *(below)* where the polar ice caps have melted and all land lies beneath the sea. Memorable moments include a crash-landing seaplane and fireballs.

7 Terminator 2: 3D

Action stunts, giant robots, and great 3D technology combine for a special-effects extravaganza as Arnold Schwarzenegger once again battles to save the world *(above)*.

ᴛᴏᴘ10 Griffith Park

Griffith Park is a 4,000-acre natural playground of rugged hills and gentle valleys, draped with native oak trees, manzanita, and sage and crisscrossed by hiking and horseback trails. The country's largest urban park owes its existence to the Welsh Griffith Jenkins Griffith (1850–1919). In 1896, Griffith donated a large portion of his estate to the city with the proviso that it become "a place of recreation and rest for the masses." Today, the park is filled with picnic areas, golf courses, and tennis courts.

Old steam locomotive, Travel Town Museum

⊝ **Griffith Park is perfect for picnics, especially in the leafy oasis of Fern Dell.** Alternatively, the Golden Spur Café at the Autry Museum serves breakfast and lunch.

⊘ **Sunset Ranch Stables (3400 Beach-wood Drive)** leads hugely popular Friday night horse-back rides through Griffith Park.

• *Map D1*
Griffith Park: Open 5am–10pm
• *Griffith Park Ranger Station: 4730 Crystal Springs Dr* • *Griffith Observatory Satellite: 4800 Western Heritage Way* • *Autry Museum of Western Heritage: 4700 Western Heritage Way*
• *Travel Town Museum: 5200 Zoo Dr* • *Bronson Caves: Follow Canyon Dr to the end, then hike up a quarter mile (400 m) past the gate just east of the last parking lot*

Top 10 Features

1 Griffith Observatory & Planetarium
2 Greek Theatre
3 Mt. Hollywood Trail
4 Merry-Go-Round
5 Los Angeles Zoo
6 Autry Museum of Western Heritage
7 Travel Town Museum
8 Forest Lawn Memorial Park – Hollywood Hills
9 Bronson Caves
10 Griffith Park & Southern Railroad

1 Griffith Observatory & Planetarium

The sparkling white observatory *(right)* has been the park's chief attraction since 1935. It's closed for renovation until early 2006, but a small satellite facility with planetarium shows and exhibits is in operation.

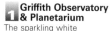

2 Greek Theatre

A favorite LA outdoor concert venue, the 1930 Greek Theatre *(above & p54)* presents a summer season of top musical talent in its leafy natural bowl setting. With just over 6,000 seats, it's great for close-ups of legends.

3 Mount Hollywood Trail

The popular trek to the top of Mount Hollywood, the highest point in Griffith Park, rewards hikers with plenty of exercise and sweeping views of Los Angeles *(below)*. Trailheads are located at Fern Dell and the Observatory.

For more information on Griffith Park log on to www.ci.la.ca.us/RAP/grifmet/griffith.htm

4 Merry-Go-Round
A slice of nostalgia in the midst of futuristic LA, this beloved 1926 Stillman carousel *(above)* has 68 exquisitely carved horses complete with real horse-hair tails.

7 Travel Town Museum
A good-sized fleet of vintage locomotives, freight and passenger cars, and several cabooses (goods trains) draw railroad aficionados to this outdoor museum. Children love riding the miniature train.

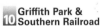

10 Griffith Park & Southern Railroad
Generations of children have boarded the three miniature trains that chug along a 1-mile (1.6-km) track *(above)* past pony rides, a Wild West ghost town, a Native American village, moving over a bridge and through a tunnel, past grazing goats and a cactus garden.

5 Los Angeles Zoo
Some 1,200 animals are found here *(above & p51)*, including koalas and chimps. The breeding program has brought the California condor back from near-extinction.

6 Autry Museum of Western Heritage
This great collection of art, artifacts, and memorabilia demystifies the history and mythology of the American West. Star exhibits include a Colt handgun collection.

8 Forest Lawn Memorial Park – Hollywood Hills
Buster Keaton and Bette Davis are among the celebrities interred in this parklike cemetery dotted with patriotic art and architecture. It was founded in 1917 by Hubert Eaton, who invented the "full-service cemetery" concept satirized by Evelyn Waugh.

9 Bronson Caves
Scenes from *Star Trek*, *Batman*, *Bonanza*, and countless other film and TV productions were shot in this former rock quarry and its caves. Tucked away in a remote corner of Griffith Park, it requires a short hike.

James Dean Memorial

James Dean was one of Hollywood's most dashing movie stars when, at age 24, he died in a car crash on a lone highway in Central California. A bronze bust outside the Griffith Park Observatory commemorates the actor, who filmed the famous knife-fight from *Rebel Without a Cause* on the steps of the building. The scene's intensity stems partly from the fact that the actors used real switchblades, though wearing protective vests. Look for Dean's bust on the west side of the lawn in front of the observatory.

Disneyland® Resort

From 1955 onwards, the landmarks of Disneyland – the Matterhorn, Sleeping Beauty's Castle, and New Orleans Square – have been as familiar and as "real" as the Eiffel Tower or the Empire State Building. In 2001, a second theme park, Disney's California Adventure™, was added adjacent to the original. Also new is Downtown Disney®, an outdoor entertainment, restaurant, and retail district. Together with the two parks and three Disney hotels, Downtown Disney forms the enormous complex called Disneyland Resort.

The Disney Matterhorn

Try the alfresco Italian at The Golden Vine Terrace in Disney's California Adventure, and Cajun fare at the candle-lit Blue Bayou in Disneyland.

If you're staying in LA and want to be first through the gate when the parks open at 8am or 9am, leave at least 90 minutes early to avoid traffic.

- Map G5
- 1313 Harbor Blvd, Anaheim, about 30 miles (48 km) south of LA
- 714-781-4565
- Seasonal hours
- www.disneyland.com
- Disneyland: 8am–10pm Mon–Fri, 8am–11pm or midnight Sat–Sun, Adm $47/$37 for adult/child 3–9
- California Adventure: 10am–6pm Mon–Fri, 10am–9pm Sat–Sun, Adm $47/$37 for adult/child 3–9
- Off-peak Disneyland: 9am–6pm Mon–Fri, 9am–8pm Sun

Top 10 Attractions

1. Pirates of the Caribbean
2. Haunted Mansion
3. Indiana Jones Adventure
4. Splash Mountain
5. Matterhorn Bobsleds
6. Big Thunder Mountain Railroad
7. Star Tours
8. Meeting Mickey
9. Roger Rabbit's Car Toon Spin
10. Autopia

1 Pirates of the Caribbean

Hold on to your hat as you plunge down into a watery world of darkness where wicked pirates plunder a Caribbean village *(right)*. Charming in spite of the low-key special effects. In New Orleans Square.

2 Haunted Mansion

Dare to enter the netherworld of this mysterious mansion in New Orleans Square inhabited by 999 ghoulish spirits. Board a "Doom Buggy" for a chilling ride and beware of hitchhiking ghosts. A perennial favorite.

3 Indiana Jones Adventure

Join Indy in his battle against the forces of evil on this bumpy adventure ride through an old temple in Adventureland. Clamped into a rickety jeep, you'll plunge into deep caverns, skirt fiery lava, and escape from being crushed by a scary giant boulder.

4 Splash Mountain

Follow Brer Rabbit and other characters from Disney's *Song of the South* as you travel along an enchanting watery path aboard hollowed-out flume logs *(left)*. The final drop will leave you gasping, exultant…and wet. In Critter Country.

Note: Prices of Disneyland tickets increase annually; discounted multi-day and multi-park passes are available

5 Matterhorn Bobsleds

The park's first roller coaster may look tame but it does manage to pack a surprising punch. Strap yourself into a double-seater bobsled for a bumpy but exhilarating race down and through the mountain, before bracing yourself for the grand finale. A must-do for kids! In Fantasyland.

9 Roger Rabbit's Car Toon Spin

Get ready for a ride on the wild side as you pilot a runaway cab through the wacky and fun world of Roger Rabbit. In Mickey's Toontown.

10 Autopia

Kids love this ride which puts them behind the wheel of two-seater sports cars for a slow but fun trip on the curvy roadways of Autopia. In Tomorrowland.

Shows, Parades, & Pyrotechnics

The thrill rides may be the main draw, but there's actually plenty else to do, especially in summer and on weekends. Daily schedules vary but may include the Disneyland Parade of the Stars, a colorful street fair featuring dozens of Disney characters and fancifully decorated floats. The skies are ablaze for Believe in the Magic, a fireworks extravaganza backed by popular songs from famous Disney movies. Another seasonal highlight is Fantasmic!, a 25-minute nighttime live action special effects show starring Mickey Mouse and other favorite Disney characters.

6 Big Thunder Mountain Railroad

Hop on to this runaway mine train roller coaster in Frontierland for a journey through the Wild West (below). Charge through bat caverns, brave falling rocks, and encounter coyotes and other scaries.

7 Star Tours

You're a space tourist headed for the moon of Endor aboard a StarSpeeder when your craft suddenly takes a wrong turn and winds up battling Darth Vader and his evil forces. A hair-raising motion simulator ride designed by George Lucas. In Tomorrowland.

8 Meeting Mickey

An audience with Mickey brings smiles to kids' faces. Before meeting Mr. Mouse up close and personal, you're invited to stroll through his house and garden and visit the set of one of his cartoons. In Mickey's Toontown.

The map you'll get with your Disneyland ticket will provide the specifics about the show schedule for the day

Left **Golden Dreams Theatre** Right **California Screamin'**

🔟 Disneyland Best of the Rest

1 Golden Dreams Theatre
In *Curtains up for California!*, a 22-minute movie, Whoopi Goldberg plays Calafia, the mythical queen that gave the state its name. She guides you through the state's history as seen through the eyes of immigrants. At Disney's California Adventure.

2 Soarin' over California
Lift off as you "fly" above the Golden Gate Bridge, Napa Valley vineyards, the Sierras, and other California landmarks in this virtual hang-gliding adventure. The most memorable ride at Disney's California Adventure.

3 It's Tough to Be a Bug
Starring a cast of termites, stinkbugs, tarantulas, and other creepy crawlies, this 3D animated movie brims with special effects, some of them rather tactile and intense. Great fun, though not for the squeamish or small children. At Disney's California Adventure.

4 California Screamin'
This scary spine-tingling roller coaster at Disney's California Adventure shoots you out like a cannon, then smoothly zooms you around the track, making a complete loop inside the head of Mickey Mouse. The "carnival meets rock'n'roll" soundtrack is a draw.

5 Grizzly River Run
Billed as the "world's highest, longest, and fastest," this thrilling whitewater raft ride takes you on a churning trip

Grizzly River Run

For reservations at Disney restaurants, call Disney Dining on 714-956-6755

The lobby of the Grand Californian Hotel

through the Sierra Nevada foothills beneath a Grizzly bear-shaped mountaintop. You will get wet on this one! At Disney's California Adventure.

6 Downtown Disney

This admission-free outdoor promenade is perfect for wrapping up the day with some shopping, a nice meal, and live music at the popular House of Blues or the Jazz Kitchen. The huge World of Disney store has all your favorite souvenirs.

7 ESPN Zone

The ultimate destination for sports junkies, this Downtown Disney fixture offers 35,000 sq ft (3,250 sq m) of nonstop action. More than 175 TV monitors sprinkled throughout broadcast different sporting events. The Sports Arena brims with sports-themed interactive, video, and virtual reality games.

8 Catal Restaurant & Uva Bar

For a culinary journey around the Mediterranean book a table at this Downtown Disney outpost of star chef Joachim Splichal.

Downstairs at the Uva Bar it's mostly casual tapas, while upstairs the focus is on fine dining. Leave room for the *crème brulée*. ✆ *1580 Disneyland Dr, Suite 103 (in Downtown Disney)* • *714-774-4442* • *Veg: On request* • *$*

9 Disney's Grand Californian

The nicest of the resort's three Disney hotels, the Grand Californian *(see p149)* carefully recreates the early 20th-century Craftsman style. The Great Hall lobby is canopied by a timbered ceiling and anchored by a large stone fireplace. A special bonus for kids and thrill seekers: a direct entry gate to Disney's California Adventure.

10 Napa Rose Restaurant

Stained glass, murals, and a cosy fireplace contribute to the refined ambience at this award-winning restaurant where dinners every evening become exciting culinary celebrations. The menu, which changes seasonally, is complemented by an exceptional wine list. At Disney's Grand Californian Hotel *(see p149)*. ✆ *1600 S Disneyland Dr* • *714-635-2300* • *Dinner only* • *$$*

For price categories of restaurants **See p79**

The Disneyland Resort

Top 10 Practical Tips

1 When to Visit
The parks are busiest in summer, and around Easter, Thanksgiving, and between Christmas and New Year. Crowds thin out from January to March and November to mid-December.

2 Beating the Crowds
If visiting during peak periods, come midweek instead of weekends and arrive at least half an hour before gates open, then head for your favorite rides first. Lines are shorter during lunchtime and the parades.

3 FastPASS System
This excellent scheme significantly cuts down on wait times in both parks. Insert your admission ticket into machines outside select attractions to receive a voucher with a pre-assigned one-hour time slot for faster boarding. It's free, but you can only have one FastPASS active at a time.

4 Saving on Admission
Discounted admission tickets for multi-day stays and multi-park visits are usually available and very useful. Check with a travel agent, area hotels, or the Disneyland website.

5 Prebooking
Buying your admission tickets in advance saves both time and effort. Try the Disney website or the ticket hotline to book beforehand.

6 Disney Hotels
Staying at one of the three official Disney hotels is not cheap but convenient for access. Disney's Grand Californian *(see p149)* even has a direct entrance to California Adventure.

7 Kids Matters
Each park has baby care centers and baby stroller rental stations. Some rides have minimum height requirements.

8 What to Wear
Wear comfortable shoes and clothes and bring a sweater or jacket if staying until after dark, even in summer.

9 What to Bring
Bring a hat, sunscreen, extra film, and whatever else you need. It's all available in the park, but at inflated prices.

10 Souvenirs
Try not to stock up on souvenirs early in the day to avoid having to carry them around. Downtown Disney's World of Disney has the best selection.

Shopping center in Downtown Disney

Top 10: Disney by Numbers

1. 450 million guests since opening
2. 1.1 million plants planted every year
3. Seven US presidents have visited
4. 1.2 million gallons of soft drinks sold annually
5. 5,000 gallons of paint used each year
6. 800 species of saplings throughout the resort
7. 21,000 employees ("cast members")
8. 4 million hamburgers consumed annually
9. 30 tons of trash collected every day
10. 100,000 light bulbs illuminate the resort

Walt Disney's Vision

Walt Disney (1901–66), the father of Mickey Mouse and other beloved cartoon characters, was a pioneer in the field of animation. A relentlessly driven and inventive man, he wished to share his brilliant imagination with families in a non-cinematic way. Watching his own children at play in a sordid amusement park, Disney was struck by his ultimate inspiration – he would build a place that was clean and filled with all kinds of attractions that parents and kids could enjoy together. Walt Disney envisioned a theme park revolving around five lands: Main Street, a setting plucked from late-19th-/early 20th-century America; Adventureland, imbued with the mystery of exotic locales; Frontierland, an homage to the pioneers; Fantasyland, a place of whimsy inspired by the song "When you Wish Upon a Star;" and Tomorrowland, with a futuristic theme fit for the budding Space Age. Disney picked a 160-acre site in Anaheim and, like the captain of a great ship, oversaw every aspect of the planning and construction of Disneyland. When the Magic Kingdom opened its gates in 1955 and 28,000 people stormed in, tears reportedly streamed down Walt Disney's cheeks – his great dream had finally become a reality.

Disneyland Opening Day

It was impossible to tell from Walt's smile, but opening day at Disneyland was close to a disaster. Temperatures soared, the parking lot asphalt bubbled, and crowds far exceeded capacity thanks to nearly 22,000 forged tickets. Rides failed, tempers flared, and it was all broadcast live! But the rest, as they say, is history.

Walt Disney with children enjoying a ride in Disneyland

Catalina Island

This island may be only 22 miles (35 km) across the sea, but it's a world away from the urban velocity of LA. Ferries dock in Mediterranean-flavored Avalon, the island's commercial hub. Most of the interior is a protected nature preserve that may only be explored on foot or bicycle (permit required), or by taking an organized tour. These are excellent ways to learn about the island's colorful history as a destination for sea otter poachers, smugglers, Union soldiers, mining speculators, and finally, tourists.

View of Avalon Harbor

🍽 Armstrong's on the bay is the best place for fresh fish, while Steve's Steakhouse scores high for meat.

🚤 The full Catalina experience should involve the water. Swimming, snorkeling, diving, kayaking, or a glass-bottom boat tour constitute great options.

Catalina is at its most pleasant in the evening after the last ferry has whisked off the day-trippers, so consider an overnight stay.

• Visitor's Bureau: Green Pleasure Pier, 310-510-1520 • Catalina Island Museum: Casino Building, 310-510-2414
• Wrigley Memorial & Botanical Gardens: 1400 Avalon Canyon, 310-510-2288 • Catalina Express: 310-519-1212 • Island Express: 310-510-2525
• Discovery Tours: 310-510-8687 • Catalina Adventure Tours: 310-510-2888 • Jeep Eco-Tours: 310-510-2595

Top 10 Features

1. Avalon Casino
2. Catalina Island Museum
3. Casino Point Marine Park
4. The Tuna Club
5. Green Pleasure Pier
6. Lover's Cove
7. Wrigley Memorial & Botanical Gardens
8. Catalina Country Club
9. Catalina Buffalo
10. Two Harbors

1 Avalon Casino
This Art Deco landmark *(above)*, built for William Wrigley Jr, opened in 1929 and was never a gambling place. It contains a movie theater and a ballroom that once hosted nationally broadcast concerts. Murals of underwater scenes adorn the exterior.

2 Catalina Island Museum
Over 7,000 years of island history come alive at this small museum in the Casino building. Highlights include locally found archaeological artifacts, pottery, and photographs from Catalina's days as the darling of Hollywood.

3 Casino Point Marine Park
Great for encounters with finned creatures, this reserve was Southern California's first city-designed water park (established in 1965). Fun for divers *(below)*.

4 The Tuna Club
The nation's oldest (1898) fishing club, it was the first to develop modern angling rules for sport-fishing. Winston Churchill and Teddy Roosevelt have been visitors here.

 Catalina Island Sportfishing (310-510-2420) operates charter fishing trips; you can fish for free from the pier

5 Green Pleasure Pier

This green pier *(left)* has been the hub of Avalon activity since 1909. For years, it was the official weighing station for tuna, marlin, and sea bass brought in by game fishing enthusiasts.

9 Catalina Buffalo

Island explorations may lead to encounters with herds of chocolate-colored buffalo. The first 14 animals were brought to Catalina in 1924 for a Zane Grey film.

10 Two Harbors

Popular with boaters, hikers, and campers, tiny Two Harbors *(left)* is a slow-paced rustic village on a natural isthmus about 23 miles (37 km) west of Avalon. It is served by ferry from the mainland and by bus from Avalon.

6 Lover's Cove

Rent a snorkel and take to the clear blue waters of this poetically named marine preserve teeming with golden Garibaldi (California's state marine fish), as well as schools of opaleyes, blue perch, and other fish.

7 Wrigley Memorial & Botanical Gardens

The monument to William Wrigley Jr, built in 1935 with local materials, lords over huge gardens *(right)*. Plants here include eight species unique to the island, including Catalina ironwood and wild tomato.

8 Catalina Country Club

In 1929, William Wrigley Jr. made Catalina the spring training ground for his baseball team. The historic clubhouse is now a restaurant *(above)*.

A Wealth of Wildlife

Catalina has a unique ecosystem, including such endemic species as the Channel Island fox and the Catalina ground squirrel. The introduction of non-native animals – such as pigs, goats, deer, and buffalo – resulted in overgrazing, a trend the Catalina Island Conservancy is seeking to reverse. Another wildlife restoration project has returned the California bald eagle to the island's skies. Pelicans, cormorants, and gulls can also be spotted. The ocean waters are abundant with sea lions, Garibaldi, flying fish, and shark.

Left **Donald Douglas, airplane designer** Right **The Los Angeles Riots (1992)**

🔟 Moments in History

1 1781: The Founding of Los Angeles

Under orders of King Carlos III of Spain, the governor of California Felipe de Neve laid out a small settlement along a river valley and, on September 4, called it El Pueblo de la Reina de Los Angeles (The Town of the Queen of the Angels), another name for the Virgin Mary *(see p71)*.

2 1850: LA Becomes a City

After the US-Mexican War ended in 1846–48, Los Angeles became part of the USA on April 4, five months before California became the 31st state. With a tiny population of about 1,600, this unruly and lawless backwater lacked even such basic urban infrastructures as graded roads and street lights.

The founding of Los Angeles

3 1876: The Arrival of the Railroad

Few events have stimulated LA's growth more than its connection to the transcontinental railroad. A small army of Chinese immigrants built the Southern Pacific railroad from Los Angeles to San Francisco. The last spike – made of gold – was driven in ceremoniously on September 5.

4 1911: The Movies Come to LA

British immigrants David and William Horsely founded Hollywood's first permanent movie studio, the Nestor Film Company, in an old tavern at the corner of Sunset Boulevard and Gower Street. Today, the site is occupied by CBS Television. Within a decade, the district had become the world's movie capital and by the 1930s and 1940s, Hollywood had officially entered its "Golden Age."

5 1913: The Opening of the LA Aqueduct

"There it is! Take it!" is how William Mulholland, father of the world's longest aqueduct, famously greeted the first spurt of water to arrive in LA from the Owens Valley, some 250 miles (400 km) north, on November 5. Even today, the Los Angeles aqueduct continues to supply over 75 percent of the water needed by the residents of this metropolis, as it is partly located in a subtropical desert.

For more on historic sites See p71

6 The 1920s: The Birth of the Aviation Industry

In possession of just $1,000, but driven by a dream, 28-year-old Donald Douglas began designing airplanes in the back of a barber shop. A year later, the first Cloudster cargo plane propelled his Douglas Aircraft Company into prominence. It went on to become one of the world's leading airplane manufacturers.

7 1965: The Watts Riots

The arrest of a young black motorist suspected of drunk driving by white policemen on August 11 sparked off six days of rioting and resulted in 34 deaths, over 1,000 injuries, and $40 million in property damage.

8 1968: The Assassination of Robert F. Kennedy

On June 5, just minutes after wrapping up a speech to celebrate his victory in the California primary, presidential candidate Robert F. Kennedy was brutally gunned down by Sirhan Sirhan.

9 1992: The LA Riots

The city erupted into violence on April 29 after the acquittal of four white police officers on trial for beating up black motorist Rodney King, an incident famously captured on videotape. The toll this time: 55 dead, 2,300 injured, and $785 million in property damage.

10 1994: Northridge Earthquake

Millions were jolted awake on January 17 by a violent earthquake measuring 6.7 on the Richter scale. It caused 57 deaths and 6,500 injuries, interrupting water, electrical, and gas services, and damaging freeways and homes.

Top 10 LA Movers & Shakers

1 Junípero Serra (1713–84)
Spanish missionary and founder of 21 California missions, including LA's Mission San Gabriel.

2 Felipe de Neve (1728–84)
The Spanish governor who founded Los Angeles in 1781.

3 Stephen Watts Kearny (1794–1848)
The American general who assisted in the capture of Los Angeles from the Mexican army in 1847.

4 Phineas Banning (1830–85)
The "Father of Los Angeles Harbor," who also constructed Southern California's first railroad in 1869.

5 William Mulholland (1855–1935)
The chief engineer of Los Angeles's Water Department.

6 Edward Doheny (1856–1935)
This miner turned multi-millionaire discovered oil near downtown LA in 1892.

7 George Freeth (1883–1916)
This Hawaiian-Irish athlete introduced surfing to Southern California in the early 1900s.

8 Harrison Gray Otis (1837–1917)
City booster and publisher of the *Los Angeles Times* for three decades.

9 D.W. Griffith (1875–1948)
Pioneering film-maker and co-founder of United Artists.

10 Tom Bradley (1917–98)
LA's first African-American mayor governed for an unprecedented five terms.

Left **Schindler House** Right **Wayfarer's Chapel**

Architectural Landmarks

1 Getty Center
The architecture of the extraordinary Getty Center is said to outshine the art displayed within its galleries. Architect Richard Meier has created an elegant, sophisticated space that is nevertheless warmly welcoming (see pp12–15).

2 Gamble House
This stunning Pasadena Craftsman bungalow marks the pinnacle of the career of Charles and Henry Greene. Built in 1908 as the retirement home of David and Mary Gamble of the Procter & Gamble family, the house has a beautiful garden, wide terraces, and open sleeping porches (see p91).

3 Schindler House
The private home and studio of Vienna-born architect Rudolf Schindler (1887–1953) is a modern architectural classic. Completed in 1922, the house's flat roof, open floor plan, ample use of glass, and rooms opening to a courtyard, greatly influenced California architecture. Today,

Gamble House

it houses the MAK Center for Arts and Architecture that hosts a year-round schedule of tours, exhibitions, lectures, and other interesting events. ◎ Map M4 • 835 N Kings Rd, West Hollywood • Open 11am–6pm Wed–Sun • Adm

4 Hollyhock House
One of Frank Lloyd Wright's masterpieces, the 1921 Hollyhock House was the architect's first LA commission. Anchoring Barnsdall Park, the avant-garde architecture of the house takes full advantage of the mild California climate. Wright created seamless transitions between indoor and outdoor space and made ample use of patios, porches, and rooftop terraces (see p97).

5 Wayfarer's Chapel
Lloyd Wright, son of Frank Lloyd Wright, set this unique glass chapel amid a grove of redwood trees on an isolated hilltop overlooking the Pacific on the Palos Verdes peninsula. Today, this fairytale structure is one of the most popular wedding venues in LA (see p119).

6 Chiat/Day Building
Reflecting architect Frank Gehry's sculptural approach to architecture, this 1991 building was commissioned by the advertising firm Chiat/Day as its West Coast corporate head-quarters. It has as its center a three-story tall pair of binoculars

Chiat/Day Building

designed by Claes Oldenburg and Coosje van Bruggen. The pile of angled rust-colored columns on the right resembles a deconstructed forest. ✎ *Map A5 • 340 Main St, Venice • Not open to public*

7 Walt Disney Concert Hall
This Frank Gehry-designed downtown extravaganza is easily recognized by its shiny and dynamically curved exterior. The new home of the Los Angeles Philharmonic Orchestra, it opened in October 2003. The city-block-sized complex also comprises two small outdoor amphitheaters *(see p54 & p72)*.

8 Chemosphere
John Lautner's bold, often experimental architectural style is perfectly exemplified in this unique private home in the Hollywood Hills. Resembling a flying saucer on a single concrete column, it was built in 1960, the same year President John F. Kennedy launched the challenge to put a man on the moon. The house was featured in Brian de Palma's 1984 movie *Body Double*. ✎ *Map D2 • 776 Torreyson Dr, Silver Lake • Not open to public*

9 Bradbury Building
The light-flooded atrium of this 1893 office building *(see p73)*, with its open-cage elevators, frilly iron work, and marble floors, is one LA's supreme architectural landmarks. Architect George Wyman allegedly accepted the job only after consulting a Ouija board. Movie buffs might recognize it from *Blade Runner* and *Chinatown*.

10 Cathedral of Our Lady of the Angels
Behind the fortresslike exterior of LA's new cathedral, designed by José Rafael Moneo, awaits a minimalist place of worship where the lack of right angles and supporting pillars creates a sense of spacious loftiness. You don't have to be a Roman Catholic to appreciate the lovely tapestries of the nave, depicting dozens of saints *(see p72)*.

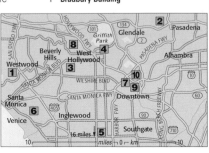

Bradbury Building

The Los Angeles Conservancy (see p138) organizes architecture-based tours on Saturday mornings

Left **Huntington Botanical Gardens** Center **Greystone Park** Right **Wrigley Mansion & Gardens**

TOP 10 Parks & Gardens

1 Huntington Library, Art Collections, & Botanical Gardens

A perfect synthesis of nature and culture, this amazing estate houses priceless collections of paintings and rare manuscripts that were started by railroad tycoon Henry E. Huntington and his wife, Arabella, in the early 19th century *(see pp22–5)*.

2 Griffith Park

The country's largest urban park *(see pp28–9)* is filled with museums, entertainment opportunities for children, hiking and horse trails, and the famous Griffith Park Observatory.

3 Greystone Park & Mansion

Popular with wedding planners and visitors in search of solitude, this secluded park affords great views of Beverly Hills. Its centerpiece is a 55-room mansion built in 1928 by oil tycoon Edward Doheny as a wedding present for his son Ned. The estate has been featured in many films, including *Air Force One*.
◈ *Map J3 • 905 Loma Vista Dr, Beverly Hills • Open May–Oct: 10am–6pm daily, Nov–Apr: 10am–5pm daily • Free • www. greystonemansion.org*

4 Virginia Robinson Gardens

The 1911 estate of department-store heiress Virginia Robinson is one of the oldest in Beverly Hills. Stroll in gardens with fountains and statuettes past towering king palms and elegant camellias flourishing in this quiet hideaway.
◈ *Map J4 • 1008 Elden Way • 310-276-5367 • Tours by appointment only • Adm*

5 Exposition Park Rose Garden

This lovely rose garden dates back to 1928 and features about 15,000 rose bushes in bloom from March to November. Great for picnics or for a respite from museum-hopping. ◈ *Map D3 • 701 State Dr • Open Apr–Dec: 9am–sunset daily • Free • www.nhm.org/expo/past/rose/main.htm*

6 Wrigley Mansion & Gardens

The winter home of William Wrigley Jr. (of Wrigley's chewing gum fame) is backed by a lovely green rose garden and now serves as the headquarters of the Pasadena Tournament of Roses Association *(see p88)*.

Virginia Robinson Gardens

For more information on LA parks log on to www.laparks.org

Palisades Park

with 70 sculptures by some of the greatest 19th- and 20th-century European and American artists, Auguste Rodin and Alexander Calder among them. ◈ *Map C2 • UCLA campus, Westwood • Open any time • Free • www.hammer. ucla.edu/collections/4*

Runyan Canyon Park

Minutes from the Walk of Fame, this small urban park has some moderately difficult trails and a colorful history – the ruins near the Fuller Steet entrance were built in 1930 by opera star John McCormack and Errol Flynn lived in one of the pool houses in the late 1950s. The Santa Monica Mountains Conservancy purchased the park in 1983. ◈ *Map N1 • At the end of Fuller St off Franklin Ave • Open until sunset (avoid after dark)*

Self-realization Fellowship Lake Shrine

Bathed in an ambience of beauty and serenity, this hidden sanctuary was created in 1950 by Paramahansa Yogananda, an Indian-born spiritual leader. Wander over to the shrine to Mahatma Gandhi or the spring-fed lake, meditate inside a recreated 16th-century windmill, or study the Court of Religions that honors all of the world's major religions. ◈ *Map B3 • 17190 Sunset Blvd • 310-454-4114 • Open 9am–4:30pm Tue–Sat, 12:30–4:30pm Sun • Free • www.yogananda-srf.org*

Palisades Park

Famous for its swaying palm trees and picture-perfect views of Santa Monica Bay (especially at sunset), Palisades Park is a playground for young and old, locals and visitors, families and courting couples. Stretching for 13 blocks atop a bluff overlooking the ocean, its benches and lawns invite picnics and people-watching. A nostalgic curiosity is the Camera Obscura inside a seniors' center. ◈ *Map C3 • Ocean Ave between Santa Monica Pier & San Vincente Blvd • Open any time • Free*

Franklin D. Murphy Sculpture Garden

Tucked away in the northeastern corner of the UCLA campus, this delightful little oasis is dotted

Left & Right **Venice Beach**

Beaches

1 Nicholas Canyon Beach
This 2-mile (3-km) lovely beach is a secret even from locals, because of its isolation and distance from the city. It hugs the base of a bluff and is a great place for those seeking solitude. Work on the tan, or sit watching the waves kiss the sand. ⌦ *33900 block of Pacific Coast Hwy, near Ventura County Line*

2 El Matador Beach
Rugged, secluded, and dotted with large boulders artistically eroded by nature, this small cliff-backed beach is one of LA's finest. Its remoteness, limited parking, and cumbersome access via a gravelly trail keep the crowds at bay. There are no facilities available, but you can explore tide pools, hide in a cave, or take a dip in the water. Clothing is optional. ⌦ *32900 block of Pacific Coast Hwy, Malibu*

3 Zuma Beach
This 2-mile (3-km) ribbon of fine, sparkling sand is one of LA's most popular beaches. Its clean water and mostly mid-sized waves are great for sports such as bodysurfing, boogie-boarding, and swimming. It teems with families and hormone-crazed teenagers on sunny summer Sundays but is nearly deserted the rest of the week, making it perfect for quiet picnics and extended walks along the beach. ⌦ *30000 block of Pacific Coast Hwy, Malibu*

4 Malibu Lagoon State/Surfrider Beach
Wedged in between the Malibu Pier and the Malibu Colony gated celebrity enclave, this popular beach offers many diversions. Watch surfers shred the waves at Surfrider Beach. The eponymous lagoon is a major stopover for migratory birds, while the nearby Adamson House with its idyllic gardens overlooks Malibu Pier and Malibu Lagoon. The house showcases pretty ceramic tiles *(see p117)*. ⌦ *Map A3 • 23200 block of Pacific Coast Hwy, Malibu*

5 Santa Monica Beach
This easy-to-access beach is one of LA's busiest. Families love the Santa Monica Pier *(see p51 & p117)* with its pretty historical carousel and amusement park. Fitness buffs can get their kicks from pedaling or skating down a paved path running past the recently restored Muscle Beach, the birthplace of the Southern California exercise craze back in the 1930s. ⌦ *Map C3 • Along Pacific Coast Hwy in Santa Monica*

Santa Monica Beach

For recorded coastal weather forecast, call 310-457-9701

Manhattan Beach

6 Venice Beach

The beach itself plays second fiddle to Venice's outlandish Ocean Front Walk, which is a magnet for freaks and those who love watching them. Against a backdrop of trinket shops and cafés, your encounters may include chainsaw jugglers, hulky musclemen, or even a singing Sikh on roller-blades *(see p118)*. ◊ *Map C3 • Ocean Front Walk between Venice Blvd & Rose Ave*

7 Manhattan Beach

The Beach Boys, who grew up around here, found inspiration for their inimitable surf music in the white sands and glorious waves of this upscale yet relaxed seaside town. Longboarders still compete for the perfect ride, especially in the area around the Manhattan Pier, which is home to an aquarium *(see p118)*. ◊ *Map C4 • West of Highland Ave*

8 Hermosa Beach

South of Manhattan Beach, Hermosa *(see p119)* has a busy bar and restaurant scene right where Pier Avenue meets the sand. Beach volleyball is the local pastime and national tournaments take place throughout the year. Only the paved South Bay Bicycle Trail that runs

from Marina del Rey to Palos Verdes lies between the sand and private homes. ◊ *Map C5 • Around Pier Ave*

9 Cabrillo Beach

The colorful sails of windsurfers flutter like giant butterflies along this beach on the breakwater of LA Harbor. Visit the nearby Cabrillo Marine Aquarium *(see p127)* to learn about marine life. ◊ *Map D6 • Stephen M. White Dr, San Pedro*

10 Seal Beach

Head to this low-key ocean playground just south of the San Gabriel River for a taste of small-town America. Warm waters and small to mid-size waves make it ideal for swimmers and surfers. A 1,865-ft (600-m) pier with a diner anchors Seal Beach. ◊ *Map F6 • Along Ocean Ave, Orange County*

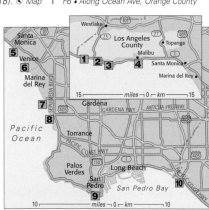

Left **Rose Bowl** Right **Hollywood Park Racetrack**

Sports & Fitness Venues

Rose Bowl
Every New Year's Day since 1923, the classic stand-off between the leading teams of college football's Pacific Coast and Big Ten conferences has taken place at this historic landmark stadium (see p88). The Bowl has also hosted five professional football Super Bowls, the 1994 World Cup soccer finals, and many other major sporting events. Its giant flea market, held every second Sunday of the month, is legendary.

Dodger Stadium
Dodger Stadium, home of the LA Dodgers major league baseball team, is widely regarded as a crown jewel among American ballparks. Completed in 1962, its clever configuration allows for good sight lines from all 56,000 seats. Panoramic city and mountain views are an extra bonus. Guided tours, which include peeks at the press box and dugout, are offered on non-game days (see p81).

Staples Center
This modern temple to professional team sports is home base for basketball's Lakers, Clippers, and Sparks, ice hockey's Kings, and indoor football's Avengers. Opened in 1999, it's also a preferred stop for blockbuster music acts à la Barbra Streisand and the Rolling Stones. Thanks to steep bleachers, views are great from most seats. ◈ Map S6 • 1111 S Figueroa St, downtown • 213-742-7300

Santa Anita Racetrack
One of the most celebrated thoroughbred racetracks in the US, Santa Anita opened in 1934 and has been a hit with Hollywood stars and the LA elite ever since. The season runs from December 26 to April. ◈ Map F1 • 285 W Huntington Dr, Arcadia • 626-574-7223 • www.santa-anita-racetrack.com

Hollywood Park Racetrack
Nicknamed the "Track of Lakes and Flowers," Hollywood Park has seen its share of triumphs since it opened in 1938. Founded by the Hollywood Turf Club under its chairman, movie mogul Jack Warner, it counted Bing Crosby and Walt Disney among its original shareholders. Thoroughbred races take place from late April to late July and again from early November to December. ◈ Map D4 • 1050 S Prairie Ave, Inglewood • 310-419-1500

Staples Center

Los Angeles Memorial Coliseum

6 Los Angeles Memorial Coliseum

An architectural triumph when completed in 1923, the Coliseum *(see p83)* in Exposition Park is now a National Historic Landmark. It first rose to prominence as a key site of the 1932 Summer Olympics and has also hosted the 1984 Games, two Super Bowls, and one World Series. Pope John Paul II has been cheered on here. ⊗ *Map D3 • 3911 South Figueroa St, Exposition Park • 213-748-6136 • www.lacoliseum.com*

7 Home Depot Center

At the core of LA's newest sports complex, opened in June 2003, is a 27,000-seat soccer stadium. It is the home turf of the Los Angeles Galaxy, the city's Major League Soccer (MLS) team, and will also serve as the US national soccer training headquarters. ⊗ *Map E5 • 18400 Avalon Blvd, Cal State Dominguez Hills campus, Carson • 310-630-2000 • www.homedepotcenter.com*

8 Yoga Works

This friendly yoga studio offers 150 classes weekly for all levels. If you don't know your downward-facing dog from your sun salutation, take an introductory class to learn about basic postures and breathing techniques. ⊗ *Map A4 • 2215 Main St (also at 1426 Montana Ave), Santa Monica • 310-393-5150 • www.yogaworks.com*

9 Crunch Gym

Vanity rules at this state-of-the-art gym famous for its celebrity clientele and innovative

Sign for Crunch Gym

workout classes. Get killer abs and buns of steel while sweating through unusual offerings such as Cardio Striptease, Kama Sutra Yoga, or Polynesian Phunk. Finish up with a relaxing session in the sauna or steam room. ⊗ *Map M3 • 8000 Sunset Blvd • 323-654-4550 • www.crunch.com*

10 Gold's Gym

Steel your biceps and other body parts in the hallowed halls once haunted by Mr. Universe himself, Arnold "The Terminator" Schwarzenegger. Other celebrity members have included Mel Gibson, Jodie Foster, and Keanu Reeves. Day passes are available. ⊗ *Map Q3 • 360 Hampton Dr, Venice • 310-392-6004 • www.goldsgym.com*

Richard Nixon Library & Birthplace

TOP 10 Drives & Day Trips

1 Mission San Fernando Rey de España

The 17th of the 21 missions founded by Franciscans in California, San Fernando was established in 1797 to supply food for El Pueblo de Los Angeles. The mission church is an exact replica of the original, destroyed in the 1971 Sylmar earthquake. The adjacent *convento* (living quarters) is the state's largest surviving adobe structure. ◉ *15151 San Fernando Mission Blvd, Mission Hills • 818-361-0186 • Open 9am–4:30pm daily • Adm*

Mission San Fernando Rey de España

2 Mission San Gabriel Archangel

Heavy flooding forced the fourth of the California missions to relocate to this spot only five years after it was founded in 1771. Though struck twice by earthquakes, the mission prospered with the help of Indian converts, many of whom are buried here. The grounds are peppered with fountains and fireplaces. A small museum has other exhibits. ◉ *Map E2 • 428 S Mission Dr, San Gabriel • 626-457-3048 • Open 9am–4:30pm daily • Adm*

3 Mulholland Drive

Named after William Mulholland, the architect of the Los Angeles aqueduct, this quintessential LA road winds for about 25 miles (40 km) along a Santa Monica Mountains ridge from Hollywood to the western San Fernando Valley. On clear days, the panoramic views are truly stunning. ◉ *Map B2*

4 Watts Towers

This folk art masterpiece is a whimsical trio of spires, adorned with rainbow-colored pieces of tile, glass, pottery, shells, and other scavenged materials. The sculpture, completed in 1954, represents the life's work of Italian immigrant Simon Rodia. Located in a high-crime neighborhood, avoid after dark. ◉ *Map E4 • 1765 E 107th St, Watts • 213-847-4646 • Half-hourly tours: 11am–2:30pm Fri, 10:30am–2:30pm Sat, 12:30–3pm Sun • Adm*

5 Six Flags Magic Mountain

The Holy Grail for roller coaster junkies, Six Flags has more ways to catapult, spin, loop, spiral, and twist than you or your stomach can imagine. Favorite white-knuckle rides include X, the world's first four-dimensional coaster, and Superman: The Escape, which has you free-falling for 6.5 seconds. ◉ *26101 Magic Mountain Parkway, Valencia • 661-255-4104 • Open May–early Sep: 10am–6pm (or later) daily; rest of the year: weekends & hols • Adm • www.sixflags.com*

6 Santa Barbara & Wine Country

This graceful "Mediterranean" town with its Spanish-style architecture and villa-studded hillsides is imbued with an unpretentious charm. With a stately mission and historical adobes, it is also a must visit for wine connoisseurs. Head for the tasting rooms of the wine country around Santa Ynez, a 45-minute drive away. ⊗ *On Hwy 101, about 90 miles (145 km) north of LA*

7 Ventura & Channel Islands National Park

Ventura's revitalized Main Street is a fun place to browse through antiques and second-hand stores and for a look inside the Mission San Buenaventura. The town is the gateway to the magnificent Channel Islands National Park. Boat excursions to the islands leave from Ventura Harbor year-round. ⊗ *On Hwy 101, about 65 miles (105 km) north of LA*

8 Laguna Beach

The picturesque setting of this friendly seaside resort has captivated artists for over a century. In summer, Laguna hosts three major art festivals, including the Pageant of the

Mission San Buenaventura church, Ventura

Recreated Oval Office, Ronald Reagan Library

Masters, which recreates well-known paintings as living tableaux using a cast of costumed locals. The Laguna Art Museum showcases vintage and contemporary California landscapes. ⊗ *On Hwy 1, about 60 miles (97 km) south of LA*

9 Richard Nixon Library & Birthplace

This memorial to the 37th US president (1913–94) includes a museum, gardens, and the restored 1910 farmhouse where he was born. High-tech exhibits focus on Nixon's achievements, but also include a gallery about Watergate. A recreation of the Lincoln Sitting Room, Nixon's favorite in the White House, is another highlight. ⊗ *18001 Yorba Linda Blvd, Yorba Linda • 714-993-3393 • Open 10am–5pm Mon–Sat, 11am–5pm Sun • Adm • www.nixonlibrary.com*

10 Ronald Reagan Library

A chunk of the Berlin Wall, a cruise missile, and a recreated Oval Office are the highlights of this museum dedicated to the 40th US president (b.1911). Exhibits trace Reagan's life from his Illinois childhood, through his Hollywood career to his political ascent, first as California governor, then as president during the waning Cold War years. ⊗ *40 Presidential Dr, Simi Valley • 800-410-8354 • Open 10am–5pm daily • Adm*

Left **California Science Center** Center **Natural History Museum** Right **Los Angeles Zoo**

🔟 LA for Children

1 Universal Studios Hollywood

This theme park attached to the world's largest movie studio is LA's biggest tourist attraction. A ticket buys a day of thrill rides and live action shows, and includes encounters with Spider-Man, the Terminator, Shrek, and other movie heroes. A must-do is the narrated tram tour to the backlot with its famous outdoor sets *(see pp26–7)*.

Shrek, Universal Studios Hollywood

2 Disneyland

Half a century after it first opened, the "Magic Kingdom" continues to be right on top of most children's must-see lists. A one-, two-, or three-day visit is guaranteed to delight, amaze, and exhaust the kids, especially since recent expansions have added a second theme park, Disney's California Adventure, and the Downtown Disney entertainment district to Disneyland *(see pp30–35)*.

3 California Science Center

Located in Exposition Park, this interactive museum makes learning about science and technology a fun experience. Feel a simulated earthquake, watch chickens hatch out of eggs, design your own car, and marvel at the inner workings of a 50-ft (15-m) long robotic doll named Tess. The adjoining Air and Space Gallery in a separate building teaches the principles of flight and space exploration *(see p81)*.

4 Natural History Museum

This engaging museum pays homage to the entire animal kingdom, including extinct species such as the perennially popular dinosaurs. Special child-oriented facilities include the Discovery Center stocked with puppets, storybooks, and a fossil-rubbing station; and the Insect Zoo, home to a host of creepy crawlies, creatures as diverse as tarantulas, centipedes, and ants *(see p81)*.

5 Long Beach Aquarium of the Pacific

Take a virtual dive through three major regions of the Pacific Ocean at this first-rate aquarium. You'll travel to the kelp beds of Southern and Baja California, the stormy shores of the northern Pacific, and the coral reefs of the tropical Pacific. Pick up laminated "dive charts" to help you identify the species, then meet some of them in the flesh *(see p128)*.

6 Los Angeles Zoo

Your kids will love the Winnick Family Children's Zoo, located within the LA Zoo. Here, they can pet barnyard animals at Muriel's Ranch, greet the zoo's newest members in the animal nursery, and dress up for interactive play and storytelling sessions at the Adventure Theater. ✪ *Map D1 • 5333 Zoo Drive • Open 10am–5pm daily • Closed 25 Dec • Adm (free for under 2s) • www.lazoo.org*

7 Cabrillo Marine Aquarium

Though small, this facility offers an entertaining introduction to life in Southern California's ocean waters. The playful yet educational exhibits are ideal for children. The staff also organize various activities, including guided tide pool walks, a marine laboratory workshop, and even "sleepovers with the fishes," when kids can "camp" out in the aquarium under staff supervision *(see p127)*.

8 Storyopolis

Creativity is king at this "city of stories." Its shelves bulge with some 5,000 kiddie books, while its walls showcase the work of top illustrators. The store is also known for its family events and storytelling sessions. ✪ *Map L5 • 116 N Robertson Blvd, W Hollywood • 310-358-2500 • Open 10am–6pm Mon–Sat, 11am–4pm Sun • Free • www.storyopolis.com*

9 Bob Baker Marionette Theater

A show at this landmark theater, founded in 1963, is truly a treat. Seated on a fluffy carpet,

Entrance to the Santa Monica Pier

children watch in wonder as the cast of marionettes and puppets sing and dance before their eyes, sometimes even interacting with them. All characters are made in the on-site workshop and many are for sale, so you can take some home with you. ✪ *Map T3 • 1345 W 1st St • 213-250-9995 • Shows: 10:30am Tue–Fri, 2:30pm Sat & Sun • Adm • www.bobbakermarionettes.com*

10 Santa Monica Pier

Pet a sea cucumber, take to the skies in a Ferris wheel, or watch local fisherfolk reel in their latest catch at this pier. These are just some of the activities on California's oldest amusement pier, whose attractions draw over three million people a year. During summer, be sure to make it to the popular free concert series that takes place on Thursday nights *(see p117)*.

Left **Rodeo Drive** Right **Melrose Avenue**

🔟 Shopping Streets

1 Main Street, Santa Monica
A laid-back yet sophisticated string of one-of-a-kind boutiques (with the occasional chain store thrown in for good measure), Main Street makes for a fun and eclectic shopping experience with plenty of cafés for people-watching. On Sundays, catch the farmers market *(see p123)*.

2 Montana Avenue
You're likely to bump into celebrities in the upscale boutiques on Montana Avenue. It's fun peeking at the clothes, home furnishings, beauty products, and exercise gear favored by fashionistas. ⊕ *Map C3 • Between 7th & 17th Sts, Santa Monica*

3 Robertson Boulevard
Price tags are steep at the boutiques on this ultra-cool two-block stretch, but you may be browsing next to celebrities such as Cameron Diaz or Jennifer Aniston. Part of the mix are cutting-edge LA designers. ⊕ *Map L5 • Between 3rd St & Beverly Blvd*

4 Rodeo Drive
A stroll along this fabled shopping street *(see p114)* is a must. All the big names in haute couture have staked out their turf on Rodeo, including Armani, Chanel, Ralph Lauren, and Versace. For better prices, walk one block east to Beverly Drive.

5 Melrose Avenue
Melrose puts the "fun" into "funky" *(see p104 & p108)*. Tattooed 20-somethings pick up vintage clothing, eccentric clubwear, and jewelry in stores between La Brea Boulevard and Fairfax Avenue. West of Fairfax is a newer designer enclave and farther west, the Pacific Design Center *(see p103)* is more about trendy home furnishings.

6 Abbot Kinney Boulevard
The pint-sized stores here teem with character, not to mention characters. This is Venice, after all: laid-back, hip, and plenty artistic. Fans of 1950s furniture, New Agers in search of aura-enhancing elixirs, and gift shoppers will find all that they want. Fairly moderate prices. ⊕ *Map A6 • Between Venice Blvd & Main St*

7 Third Street Promenade
A carnival atmosphere reigns on this popular pedestrian-only strip, especially in summer.

Main Street, Santa Monica

Check out Fantasies Come True at 8012 Melrose Avenue for Hollywood memorabilia

Third Street Promenade

Upscale chains such as Banana Republic and Urban Outfitters dominate with a few bookstores and old-timers such as the Puzzle Zoo game thrown in *(see p117).*

8 West Third Street

Wedged in between the Beverly Center and the Original Farmers Market, this mile-long strip is one of the hippest shopping scenes in LA. The bounty ranges from unconventional gift stores such as Raena to LA-made fashions at Seaver and international beauty products at Palmetto. ✪ *Map M5 • Between La Cienega Blvd & Fairfax Ave, W Hollywood*

9 Santee Alley

Bargain hunters will love this pedestrian-only lane, the busiest in the Fashion District and the center of LA's garment industry. In a setting reminiscent of an Oriental bazaar, vendors hawk cut-rate clothing, accessories, and luggage. Alas, name-brand knock-offs are not uncommon, so beware. ✪ *Map T6 • Between Olympic Blvd & 12th St, downtown*

10 Old Town Pasadena

Once an ancient crumbling historic district, Old Town Pasadena was given a makeover in the 1990s. Today, Colorado Boulevard and its side streets offer a pleasant shopping experience in mostly mid-priced chains and specialty stores *(see p87).*

Top 10 Shopping Malls

1 The Grove at Farmers Market

Outdoor mall with mock streetscape and fountains *(see p103).* ✪ 323-900-8000

2 Beverly Center

Upscale retail assortment within a fortress-like façade. ✪ *Map L5 •* 310-854-0070

3 Santa Monica Place

Frank Gehry-designed mall with great food courts. ✪ *Map A4 •* 310-394-5451

4 Glendale Galleria

Dedicated mall-crawlers will love this heaven of over 250 mostly mid-priced stores. ✪ *Map E1 •* 818-240-9481

5 Westside Pavilion

Neighborhood mall with attractive glass-roof design and art house movie theater. ✪ *Map C3 •* 310-474-6255

6 Westfield Shoppingtown Century City

Elegant shopping area with boutiques and valet parking. ✪ *Map C2 •* 310-553-5300

7 Paseo Colorado

Trendy Pasadena "urban village" with 65 stores and Mediterranean architecture. ✪ *Map F1 •* 626-795-8891

8 Hollywood & Highland

Shop beneath the Hollywood Sign at this fanciful outdoor mall in Tinseltown. ✪ *Map P2 •* 323-467-6412

9 Westfield Shoppingtown Fashion Square

Indoor mall that prides itself on outstanding service. ✪ *Map C1 •* 818-783-0550

10 7th+Fig

Fun architecture, great food, and a colorful farmers market on Thursdays. ✪ *Map T5 •* 213-955-7150

Left **Music Center** Center **Pantages Theatre** Right **Greek Theatre**

🔟 Performing Arts Venues

1 Hollywood Bowl
Concerts beneath the stars at this natural amphitheater are a beloved summer tradition. The range extends from Beethoven to the Beatles, cabaret to rock. Enjoy a picnic before the show. Cheap tickets are available for some shows *(see p95)*.

2 Music Center
This three-venue arts center represents LA culture. The LA Opera, directed by Plàcido Domingo, makes its home at the Dorothy Chandler Pavilion, while cutting-edge plays are presented at the Ahmanson Theater and the Mark Taper Forum. *Map V4 • 135 N Grand Ave, Downtown • 213-972-7211*

3 Walt Disney Concert Hall
This Frank Gehry creation, the newest part of the Music Center, features cleverly designed seating which makes listening to the LA Philharmonic Orchestra, playing beneath the sail-like ceiling of the hall, an unforgettable experience *(see p41 & p72)*.

4 Ford Amphitheatre
Built in 1920 and embraced by the Hollywood Hills, this intimate outdoor amphitheater presents a multicultural program of music, dance, film, and theater events. *Map P1 • 2580 Cahuenga Blvd E • 323-461-3673 • www.fordamphitheatre.org*

5 Greek Theatre
Tucked into a hillside in Griffith Park, the popular Greek Theatre *(see p28)* has featured such musical greats as B.B. King. Stars leave their handprints on the Wall of Fame. *Map D2 • 2700 N Vermont Canyon • 323-665-1927 • www.greektheatrela.com*

6 Universal Amphitheatre
Next to Universal Studios and Universal City Walk, this state-of-the-art indoor music venue draws up to 6,300 people with a star-studded calendar of events that have included Fleetwood Mac and Sheryl Crow. *Map D2 • 100 Universal City Plaza, Universal City • 818-777-3931 (box office)*

Hollywood Bowl

  For the latest information, log on to www.musiccenter.org (Music Center)

Royce Hall, UCLA

7 Pantages Theatre
This Art Deco jewel *(see p11)* was recently restored to its 1929 glory. Once a movie palace, its eye-popping auditorium hosted the Academy Awards from 1949–59. ◈ *Map Q2 • 6233 Hollywood Blvd • www.nederlander.com*

8 Kodak Theatre
For the first time in 42 years, the Academy Awards took place in Hollywood, when the Kodak hosted it in 2002. This entertainment venue also boasts the distinction of possessing one of the world's largest stages. ◈ *Map P2 • 6801 Hollywood Blvd • 323-308-6363 • Half-hourly tours: 10:30am–2:30pm daily • Adm • www.kodaktheatre.com*

9 Royce Hall
One of UCLA's original buildings, the 1929 Romanesque Royce Hall *(see p112)* once hosted greats such as George Gershwin. Today, the hall presents an avant-garde calendar of dance, music, and theater events. ◈ *Map C2 • UCLA Campus, Westwood • 310-825-2101 • www.uclalive.org*

10 Theatricum Botanicum
This lovely venue was the brainchild of Will Geer, best known for his portrayal of Grandpa in the 1970s TV series *The Waltons*. Watch popular classics. ◈ *Map B2 • 1419 N Topanga Canyon Blvd • 310-455-3723 • www.theatricum.com*

Top 10 Comedy Clubs

1 The Laugh Factory
Features big name acts and promising newcomers of all ethnic backgrounds. ◈ *8001 Sunset Blvd • 323-656-1336*

2 The Groundlings
TV star Lisa Kudrow (of the TV series *Friends*) graduated from here. ◈ *7307 Melrose Ave • 323-934-4747*

3 The Improv
Robin Williams has tickled funny bones at this famous haunt with eatery. ◈ *8162 Melrose Ave • 323-651-2583*

4 Improv Olympic West
LA branch of famous Chicago original. ◈ *6366 Hollywood Blvd • 323-962-7560*

5 Comedy Store
Legendary club launched the careers of Jim Carrey and Michael Keaton. ◈ *8433 Sunset Blvd • 323-656-6225*

6 Bang Improv Studios
Veteran improv actors perform low-cost, high-energy shows in a tiny space with campy decor. ◈ *457 N Fairfax Blvd • 323-653-6886*

7 ACME Comedy Theater
Presents the best troupe for sketch comedy in LA in its own theater. ◈ *135 N La Brea Ave • 323-525-0202*

8 The Comedy & Magic Club
Famous comics including Jay Leno (on most Sundays) try out new material here. ◈ *1018 Hermosa Ave • 310-372-1193*

9 The Ice House
One of the US's oldest comedy clubs. ◈ *24 N Mentor Ave, Pasadena • 626-577-1894*

10 Ha Ha Café
This club nurtures budding comics. ◈ *5010 Lankershim Blvd • 818-508-4995*

A great source of discount tickets (but available only on the day of the performance) is Theater LA (see p140)

Left **ArcLight Cinemas & Cinerama Dome** Right **El Capitan Theatre**

Movie Theaters

Pacific Theatres at the Grove

1 Pacific Theatres at The Grove

State-of-the-art meets Art Deco charm, with gloved ushers helping you to your seat. Pay a little more and get a chair on the mezzanine level with snack service. ⊗ *Map N5 • 189 The Grove Drive, Midtown • 323-692-0164*

2 The Bridge

This cutting-edge theater has been subtitled "cinema de lux" for very good reason. Enjoy recently released movies sitting in large and luxurious leather chairs. ⊗ *Map D3 • 6081 Center Dr, off Fwy 405 • 310-568-3375*

3 ArcLight Cinemas & Cinerama Dome

The exquisite 14-screen ArcLight is the shiny new neighbor of the futuristic Cinerama Dome *(see p96)*. ArcLight's lobby, lorded over by a giant digital board, leads to a lively café-bar with terrace. ⊗ *Map Q3 • 6360 W Sunset Blvd • 323-464-4226*

4 El Capitan Theatre

Old-time Hollywood glamour has returned to LA courtesy of the Walt Disney Corporation, which restored this 1926 theater *(see p11)*. It functions as a first-run cinema showing Disney flicks, sometimes preceded by lavish live shows. ⊗ *Map P2 • 6838 Hollywood Blvd • 323-467-7674*

5 Mann's Chinese Theatre

This flashy 1927 Chinese fantasy palace *(see p11)* is still the site of movie premieres. Catch a blockbuster here – you never know which famous name might be sitting next to you. Note that the sixplex next door to the theater has none of the original's historic flair. ⊗ *Map P2 • 6925 Hollywood Blvd • 323-464-6266*

6 The Egyptian Theatre

This oldest of Hollywood Boulevard's themed 1920s movie palaces *(see p11)* houses the

American Cinematheque. It presents art house fare and the documentary *Forever Hollywood* on weekends. Regular events feature famous directors and actors. ⊗ *Map P2 • 6712 Hollywood Blvd*

7 Silent Movie Theatre

The movies of Charlie Chaplin, Rudolph Valentino, and other silent era legends

Mann's Chinese Theatre

For other entertainment venues See pp54–5 & pp60–61

regularly reel off at the nation's only remaining silent movie theater. Live music from the 1920s and classic cartoons often precede screenings. ◎ *Map M4* • *611 N Fairfax Ave, Midtown* • *323-655-2520* • *www.silentmovietheater.com*

8 The Nuart Theatre
One of Los Angeles's finest independent theaters shows the kind of experimental and foreign fare that most multiplexes would avoid. The cult classic *The Rocky Horror Picture Show* still runs every Saturday. ◎ *Map C3* • *11272 Santa Monica Blvd* • *310-281-8223* • *www.landmarktheaters.com*

9 Bing Theater at LACMA
LA's famous art museum *(see pp16–19)* presents high-brow retrospectives of a particular actor or director in its on-site theater with a top-notch digital sound system. On Tuesdays at 1pm, catch classic films for a small fee. ◎ *Map N6* • *5905 Wilshire Blvd, Midtown* • *323-857-6010* • *www.lacma.org*

10 California Science Center IMAX Theater
IMAX stands for "maximum image" and with a screen that is seven stories tall and 90-ft (27-m) wide, it's a fitting name. The giant screen with its six-channel surround-sound system ensures total sensorial immersion *(see p81)*. ◎ *Map D3* • *700 State Dr, Exposition Park* • *323-724-3623* • *www.casciencectr.org*

California Science Center

Top 10 Oscar Facts

1 How the Oscar got its Name
The statuette got its name in 1931 after future Academy executive director Margaret Herrick remarked that it resembled her uncle Oscar.

2 Oscar by Numbers
The 13.5-in (34-cm) tall, 8.5-lb (3.8-kg) Oscar has been handed out over 2,400 times.

3 Top Three Oscar-winning Films
Ben Hur and *Titanic* tie the number one spot (11 awards each), while *West Side Story* comes in third with ten.

4 Actor with Most Oscars
A tie – both Walter Brennan and Jack Nicholson won three times.

5 Actress with Most Oscars
Katherine Hepburn, who won the Oscar four times.

6 All-time Oscar Winner
Walt Disney – 26 awards.

7 Youngest Oscar Winner
Shirley Temple, who was six years and 310 days old.

8 Oscar Controversy
In 1972, Marlon Brando refused the Best Actor award in protest against the US government's mistreatment of Native Americans.

9 Oscar Venues
The Hollywood Roosevelt Hotel, Ambassador Hotel, Shrine Auditorium, Pantages Theatre, and The Kodak (current) are the famous ones.

10 Oscar Parties
The official post-award Governor's Ball held at many venues since 1957, moved to the Hollywood and Highland Grand Ballroom in 2002.

 For more on Hollywood **See pp10–11 & pp58–9**

Left **The NBC tour brochure cover** Right **Sam French Theatre & Film Bookshop**

🔟 Hollywood Connections

1 Warner Bros Tour
This excellent two-hour tour provides a thorough look at both the glamorous history as well as the day-to-day working reality of a major motion picture studio. Watch an introductory movie, visit the museum, and outdoor sets. Actual tour routes depend on that day's production schedule. ⊗ *Map D1 • 4000 Warner Blvd, Burbank • 818-846-1403 • Adm • www.wbtours.com*

2 Sony Pictures Studio Tour
This giant movie lot was the historic home of the famous MGM, producer of well-known classics such as *The Wizard of Oz*, until purchased by Sony in 1990. The two-hour walking tour may include visits to the set of the game show *Jeopardy*, the wardrobe department, and an exciting trip to the sound studio. ⊗ *Map C3 • 10202 W Washington Blvd, Culver City • 323-520-8687 • Tours: Call for schedule, reservations required • Adm*

3 NBC Tour
This tour offers an affordable look at the inner workings of a major TV production studio. A highlight is a visit to the set of Jay Leno's *The Tonight Show*. Call in advance or check the website to find out how to be part of the studio audience. ⊗ *Map D1 • 3000 W Alameda Ave, Burbank • 818-840-3537 • Hourly tours: 9am–3pm Mon–Fri • www.nbc.com • Adm*

4 Audiences Unlimited
A great way to see stars live is to be part of a studio audience. This organization handles the distribution of free tickets to live tapings, primarily of game shows and sitcoms. Book early for the best selection. ⊗ *Map D2 • 100 Universal City Plaza building • 818-753-3470 (ext 812) • www.tvtickets.com*

5 Larry Edmunds Bookshop
Books about animation, acting, and Hollywood history – Larry Edmunds' fabulous store

Warner Bros Studio, Burbank

For information on Hollywood, drop by the Hollywood Visitors' Information Center at Janes House Square, 6541 Hollywood Blvd has it all, as well as historic movie posters, publicity stills, and screenplays. ✪ *Map P2* • *6644 Hollywood Blvd* • *323-463-3273* • *www.larryedmunds.com*

6 Samuel French Theatre & Film Bookshop

This purveyor of printed Hollywood material is geared to the needs of professional actors and screenwriters. The company also publishes and leases scripts of live plays. ✪ *Map N3* • *7623 Sunset Blvd* • *323-876-0570* • *www.samuelfrench.com*

7 American Cinematheque

To listen to Hollywood actors and directors discuss movies, attend screenings by this group headquartered at the historic Egyptian Theatre *(see p11 & p56)*. The schedule ranges from retrospectives to filmmaker tributes.

8 Margaret Herrick Library

It's easy to get lost in this vast repository of movie-related books and publications, operated by the Academy of Motion Picture Arts and Sciences. ✪ *Map L6* • *333 S La Cienega Blvd, Beverly Hills* • *310-247-3020* • *Open 10am–6pm Mon, Tue, Thu, & Fri* • *Free (ID required)*

9 It's a Wrap!

Much of the clothing worn by actors ends up here after the the final shot (when the director shouts "It's a wrap!"). There are bargains galore and each item sports a tag identifying the show it appeared on. ✪ *Map D1* • *3315 W Magnolia Blvd, Burbank* • *818-567-7366* • *www.itsawraphollywood.com*

10 Reel Clothes & Props

On sale here are pricey, collectible clothes worn by the biggest stars. A fun collection of props are also available. ✪ *Map Q2* • *5525 N Cahuenga Blvd, N Hollywood* • *818-508-7762* • *www.reelclothes.com*

Top 10 LA Scandals

1 Fatty Arbuckle
Silent era funnyman was charged with the murder of actress Virginia Rappe in 1921, thus ending his career.

2 Errol Flynn
Hard-living swashbuckler whose penchant for teenage girls earned him a statutory rape charge in 1942.

3 Lana Turner
The actress's mobster lover was found stabbed to death in her house in 1958. Her teenage daughter, Cheryl Crane, took the blame.

4 Sharon Tate
Tate, 8 1/2 months pregnant, was among the victims of the Charles Manson murders in 1969.

5 John Belushi
A drug overdose ended this Blues Brother's life at age 33 in 1982 at the Chateau Marmont Hotel.

6 O.J. Simpson
The football star was cleared of the murder of his wife and her friend in 1994.

7 Heidi Fleiss
Infamous Hollywood madame, who ran an elite call-girl racket, received 37 months in jail in 1997.

8 George Michael
Pop singer was sentenced to a fine and community service in 1998 for lewd behavior in public.

9 Hugh Grant
Caught in the sexual act with a prostitute in his car, he was given two years' probation and a fine.

10 Winona Ryder
Actress convicted in 2002 of shoplifting $5,500 worth of goods; got probation, community service, and a fine.

 Call up Celebrity Tours, in Palm Springs, at 888-805-2700 for a look at the lives of the area's most exclusive residents

59

Left **The Derby neon sign** Right **The Largo sign**

TOP 10 Live Music Clubs

Catalina Bar & Grill

1 Catalina Bar & Grill

One of LA's finest jazz clubs, this snug venue has booked major talents, including jazz royalty such as Dizzy Gillespie. Photographs of jazz legends adorn the room, which serves Continental cuisine. Two-drink minimum for non-diners. ✆ Map P3 • 6725 Sunset Blvd, Hollywood • 323-466-2210 • Open daily • www.catalinajazzclub.com

2 The Derby

This glamorous venue became the center of the swing dance revival in the 1990s after being featured in the movie *The Swingers*. There's still plenty of jivin', and swing lessons at least twice weekly (usually Monday and Saturday), while hip hop, house, and other sounds draw crowds on remaining nights. ✆ Map D2 • 4500 Los Feliz Blvd • 323-663-8979 • Open daily • www.the-derby.com

3 Conga Room

Backed by Jennifer Lopez and other celebrities, this club presents Latin and world music, with an emphasis on salsa, to a multicultural crowd. Free salsa lessons. ✆ Map P6 • 5364 Wilshire Blvd, Midtown • 323-938-1696 • Open Thu–Sat • www.congaroom.com

4 McCabe's Guitar Shop

The biggest names in folk music from Arlo Guthrie to Al Viola have played in the back room of this legendary acoustic instruments store. The no-frills, convivial setting appeals to true devotees. Moderate ticket prices and free coffee. ✆ Map C3 • 3101 Pico Blvd, Santa Monica • 310-828-4497 • Shows: usually Fri, Sat, & Sun • www.mccabes.com

5 The Troubadour

Catch local and touring bands on their way to greatness – Elton John and Sheryl Crow have played here. The upstairs balcony offers good stage views and there are three bars. ✆ Map K4 • 9081 Santa Monica Blvd, West Hollywood • 310-276-6168 • Open daily

McCabe's Guitar Shop façade

6 Largo

Talking during performances is strictly forbidden at this sit-down club. Listen to musicians from different genres. Without dinner reservations it's standing room only on a space available basis. Mondays are comedy nights. ◈ Map M4 • 432 N Fairfax Ave, Midtown/ Hollywood • 323-852-1073 • Open daily

7 Blue Café

This lively Long Beach venue fronted by a big patio books some of the best blues per-formers around. Catch emerging talent during the weekday Happy Hours (4–8pm), or hang around for the main show at 10pm. ◈ Map E6 • 210 The Promenade, North Long Beach • 562-983-7111 • Open Tue–Sun

8 Babe & Ricky's Inn

If this club is the heart of the LA blues scene, Laura Mae Gross is its soul. Since 1964, she has nurtured new talent and hosted greats such as B.B. King. Monday's jam nights (with free fried chicken) are legendary. ◈ Map D3 • 4339 Leimert Blvd, Liemert Park • 323-295-9112 • Open Thu–Mon • www.bluesbar.com

9 Feinstein's at the Cinegrill

This nightclub recently reopened as a chic supper club with a musical menu of cabaret and jazz. Named after singer-pianist Michael Feinstein, it's an intimate venue with a great sound. ◈ Map P2 • 7000 Hollywood Blvd • 323-466-7000 • Open Tue–Sat

10 Club Spaceland

Night after night, Club Spaceland hosts LA's edgiest, most creative, and occasionally, most bizarre rock talent in front of a grungy crowd. ◈ Map D2 • 1717 Silver Lake Blvd • 323-661-4380 • Open daily • www.clubspaceland.com

Top 10 Hotel Bars

1 W Bar

Sexy socialites and their beaus drape themselves around the sleek bar at the W Los Angeles (see p147).

2 Cameo Bar

Hollywood glamour goes seaside at this Neo-Colonial bar at the Viceroy (see p147).

3 The Bar at the Hotel Bel-Air

Soft lighting, music, and a crackling fireplace provide the perfect romantic backdrop at this luxury bar (see p144).

4 Rooftop Bar at The Standard Downtown

Ultra-cool spot with bird's-eye city views and unique water-beds for lounging (see p147).

5 Windows Lounge

Celebrity sightings are common at this swank bar at the Four Seasons (see p144).

6 Bar at The Argyle

Order martinis at this Sunset Strip haven with a decor reminiscent of Holly-wood's Golden Era (see p146).

7 Blue on Blue

Hobnob with the sassy, fashionable crowd while sipping a signature Blue Avalon (see p147).

8 Toppers

An outside glass elevator whisks you to this sports bar in the Radisson-Huntley Hotel. ◈ Map A3 • 1111 2nd St, Santa Monica • 310-393-8080

9 Gallery Bar

A dark and quiet spot to unwind with cocktails in old-world grandeur at the stylish Biltmore (see p77).

10 The Whiskey Bar

The door policy might be tight, but you'll be mingling with celebs at the Sunset Marquis (see p65 & p147).

Left **Angelyne Billboards** Right **Million Dollar Pharmacy**

🔟 Weird & Wacky LA

1 Angelyne Billboards
One of Hollywood's biggest icons is not an actress, singer, or model. She's Angelyne, the self-proclaimed "Love Goddess of Hollywood," famous for showing off her gravity-defying physical attributes on giant billboards. Occasionally spotted driving around town in her pink Corvette, Angelyne enjoys a worldwide fan club and has been featured in movies and countless articles.

2 Necromance
If the sight of freeze-dried ducklings gives you the creeps, you should probably avoid this "little shop of horrors." Budding sorcerers and those in search of decorations for their own haunted mansions will find delightfully macabre stuff to buy. ◈ Map P4
• 7220 Melrose Ave • 323-934-8684
• www.necromance.com

3 Dennis Woodruff
Dennis Woodruff is best known for being a non-celebrity. The "world's most famous

Necromance

unknown actor" can be seen around Hollywood in his outra-geous vintage car decorated with lines such as "Buy my movie" or "Actor Awaiting his Break." Wood-ruff's elusive quest for fame was featured in Angelo Guglielmo's documentary *Idling Brando*.

4 Porno Walk of Fame
LA lays claim to the rather dubious title of "World Capital of the Adult Entertainment Indus-try." Its biggest legends of lust, including John Holmes and Linda Lovelace, have left their hand- and footprints in the sidewalk outside the former Pussycat movie theater. Renamed the Tomkat Theater, it now shows gay porn. ◈ Map N3 • 7734 Santa Monica Blvd, Hollywood • 323-650-9551

5 Skeletons in the Closet
Fancy a beach towel with a dead body outline? A coffee mug featuring a skeleton dressed up like Sherlock Holmes? A toe tag key chain? You'll find all these and more at this tongue-in-cheek gift shop operated by the LA County Coroner and located right above the morgue. Proceeds benefit a county-run youth drunk driver alternative sentencing program. ◈ Map E2 • 1104 N Mission Rd, E of Downtown • 323-343-0760
• www.lacoroner.com

6 Million Dollar Pharmacy
The aisles of this bizarre "pharmacy" are packed with potions and powders said to cure

Find out more about Angelyne at www.angelyne.com/tc.html

many ills, mostly of the aching heart variety. Wiping your floors with a vile liquid will banish evil spirits, while lighting a strange-smelling candle will bring you good fortune. They also have voodoo dolls, complete with an instruction leaflet, should you feel really wicked. ✆ Map V4 • 301 S Broadway, Downtown • 213-687-3688

7 Farmer John Mural
It takes a morbid sense of humor to cover a sausage factory with a giant mural of verdant pastures with happy, frolicking pigs. But that's just what the Cloughertys, the family behind the Farmer John meat empire, did when they hired Les Grimes, a Hollywood set painter, in the late 1950s. Tourists have gone "hog-wild" ever since. ✆ Map E3 • 3049 E Vernon Ave, southwest of Downtown

8 Banana Museum
Ken Bannister is so bananas over the yellow fruit that he has collected 17,000 banana-themed items and even earned an entry in the Guinness Book of Records. Arranged in a rather haphazard fashion in his tiny storefront "museum" are bananas made of plastic, glass, plus toys, T-shirts, tobacco, and even a petrified banana! ✆ Map F1 • 2424 N El Molino Ave, Altadena • 760-242-6724 • Open by appointment only

9 Museum of Jurassic Technology
The doors of this bizarre museum open up a parallel universe where the seemingly mundane becomes extraordinary. Exhibits

Venice Boardwalk

include Cameroonian stink ants and American trailer park populations alongside an uncanny likeness of Pope John Paul II in the eye of a needle. Give in to this strange world and prepared to be mesmerized. ✆ Map C3 • 9341 Venice Blvd, Culver City • 310-836-6131 • Open 2–8pm Thu, noon–6pm Fri–Sun • Donation • www.mjt.org

10 Venice Boardwalk
Venice's origins as an amusement park live on along the Venice Boardwalk. An endless parade of poseurs and eccentrics, from wiry street performers dancing on broken glass to steroid-enhanced musclemen, it remains a place where true freedom of expression reigns (see p122).

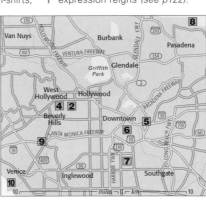

Left **Viper Room** Right **Spago Beverly Hills**

Places to See & Be Seen

1 Fred Segal
Today's hottest stars such as Jennifer Aniston, Nicole Kidman, and George Clooney have all been spotted browsing for cool clothes and accessories at this style emporium. It's also a favorite for wardrobe buyers for TV and feature films. The West Hollywood branch is more celebrity-heavy *(see p108)*.

2 Urth Café
This West Hollywood eating joint is a health- and waist-conscious café on the celebrity radar, but most days it's just the usual in-crowd munching on vegetarian lasagne and noshing on New York cheesecake. The sunny patio offers the best vantage point for checking out the crowd from behind sunglasses. ◈ *Map L4 • 8565 Melrose Ave, West Hollywood • 310-659-0628*

3 Viper Room
Celebrities like to hang out with their own kind, so it's no wonder that the VIP booths at this Johnny Depp-owned nightclub are often filled with his personal pals. Occasionally, stars such as Bruce Springsteen or the Wallflowers take to the stage, but these coveted concerts are rarely advertised *(see p9 & p106)*.

4 The Ivy
The air at this rustic French restaurant is electric with the buzz of Hollywood's power players. Deals are struck daily between movie moguls, celebs, agents, and their high-profile clients. Count yourself fortunate if you manage to score a table on the fenced-in patio table for great people and celeb watching. ◈ *Map L5 • 113 N Robertson Blvd, West Hollywood • 310-274-8303*

Fred Segal

Spago Beverly Hills

5 There aren't too many restaurants whose owners are as famous as their A-list patrons, but Wolfgang Puck is certainly one of them. He can often be seen schmoozing in the dining room and blowing air kisses. One of the most pleasant spots for stargazing (see p67 & p115).

Book Soup

6 This excellent independent bookstore draws a sizeable celebrity contingent with its eclectic offerings, including international publications. Try and increase your chances of meeting a star by attending one of their book readings or book signing sessions. Call for schedules.
Ⓢ Map L3 • 8818 Sunset Blvd, West Hollywood • 310-659-3110

The Whiskey Bar

7 Catering to a "Rolls-Royce" rock'n'roll crowd, this hot hangout at the Sunset Marquis Hotel (see p61 & p147) is owned by Rande Gerber, husband of supermodel Cindy Crawford. Getting past the velvet rope isn't easy, especially when big names such as Bono from U2 come by.

Barneys New York

8 Max out your credit card while keeping an eye out for superstars and celebrities at this luxurious department store. All the major designers from Armani to Helmut Lang and Dolce & Gabbana are represented here. Take in the nice views from the outdoor tables in the rooftop deli.
Ⓢ Map J6 • 9570 Wilshire Blvd, Beverly Hills • 310-276-4400

The Staples Center

LA Lakers Games at Staples Center

9 The Los Angeles Lakers, the city's fabled basketball team, always attract a fair number of celebrities to its games at the Staples Center (see p46). Number One fan, Jack Nicholson, can usually be spotted courtside, and Denzel Washington and Eddie Murphy are regulars. Leonardo DiCaprio, Jennifer Lopez, and Ben Affleck have also made appearances.

Chateau Marmont & Bar Marmont

10 Celebrities have flocked to this European-style hotel like moths to the flame since its opening way back in 1929. Famed for its discretion, it has remained a favorite spot for celebrity trysts. Check out the chic Bar Marmont (see p8, p106, & p146).

Left **Lobster on display in Water Grill** Right **Ciudad**

Restaurants

The Patina sign

1 Patina

A long-time darling of food critics and gourmets, Patina is where star chef Joachim Splichal takes his innovative French-California cuisine to new heights. The melt-in-your-mouth *côte de boeuf*, served table-side, is indicative of the kitchen's lofty aspirations. Try the chef's superb tasting menu. ⊗ *Map U4 • Walt Disney Concert Hall, 141 S Grand Ave • 213-972-3331 • $$$$*

2 Water Grill

A premier seafood joint, this is usually packed to the gills with patrons appreciative of the dock-fresh fare and superb service. Chef Michael Cimarusti turns each dish into a culinary celebration of bold flavors and pleasing textures. The yummy white clam chowder and hand-cut tuna tartare are outstanding, and the oyster bar scores high with the pre-theater crowd *(see p79)*.

3 Ciudad

Settle down with a *mojito* (a minty rum drink) beneath the skyscrapers at one of downtown's liveliest dining rooms. The menu blends the exotic flavors and ingredients of several Latin American cuisines into intriguing new dishes. The inexpensive *cuchifrito* (snack) menu served in the afternoon at the bar is great for sampling *(see p79)*.

4 Campanile

Chefs Mark Peel and Nancy Silverton are the royal couple on LA's cuisine scene. Both have garnered multiple awards, he for his pioneering "urban rustic" fare, and she for her scrumptious breads and divine desserts. This long-running restaurant is a definite highlight on LA's culinary scene *(see p109)*.

5 Matsuhisa

This is the original of a small chain of restaurants serving Nobu Matsuhisa's inspired Japanese-Peruvian fusion fare. The sushi is impeccable and the tempura extra-light, but the chef's talent really lies in cooked seafood dishes, many paired with Nobu's perky sauces. Celebrity sightings

Spago Beverly Hills

 *For more restaurants and a key to price categories **See pp79, 85, 93, 101, 109, 115, 125, 131***

are likely. Make reservations several days in advance to avoid the rush *(see p115)*.

6 Spago Beverly Hills

This beautiful Wolfgang Puck outpost is a favorite with the rich and famous and a great place to sample California cuisine. The chef keeps the menu in flux but always pairs supreme cuts of meat or fish with seasonal side dishes such as chanterelle mushrooms. The lox pizza is always popular. Early reservations essential *(see p65 & p115)*.

7 Michael's

A pioneer of California cuisine, Michael's serves Oscar-worthy cuisine in a luscious garden setting, making it one of the best alfresco dining spots in all LA. The food delights eye and palate. ⊗ *Map A3 • 1147 3rd St, Santa Monica • 310-451-0843 • Dis. access • Accepts credit cards • Veg: Yes • $$$*

8 Bastide

Helmed by Alain Giraud, one of LA's star chefs, this chic eatery transports you to the sunny climes of Southern France. Seated in the delightful tree-fringed garden, patrons linger over plates of sautéed *foie gras* or other upscale indulgences, accompanied by exquisite French wine. ⊗ *Map L4 • 8475 Melrose Place, W Hollywood • 323-651-5950 • Dis. access • Accepts credit cards • Veg: Yes • $$$$*

9 Joe's

Joe Miller is one of LA's most dedicated and competent chefs, and his excellent French-infused California cuisine has leagues of loyal fans. Using only fresh,

Entrance to Joe's

seasonal ingredients, Miller shows off his far-reaching talent with frequently changing menus. The *prix fixe* dinners are good value, while lunches are a real steal. Dinner reservations are a must to avoid disappointment later *(see p125)*.

10 Valentino

For over 30 years, Piero Selvaggio has delighted diners with his charm and inspired Italian cuisine. His 150,000 plus cellar of handpicked wines from all regions of the Boot is outstanding. So are the ingredients, many of them imported from the old country. Insiders ignore the menu and try the "extravaganza," a series of delicious treats. ⊗ *Map C3 • 3115 Pico Blvd, Santa Monica • 310-829-4313 • Dis. access • Accepts credit cards • Veg: Yes • $*

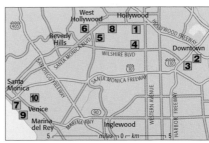

Following pages **Rush-hour traffic, downtown Los Angeles**

67

AROUND TOWN

LOS ANGELES TOP 10

Left **Olvera Street marketplace, El Pueblo de Los Angeles** Right **Union Station**

Downtown

DOWNTOWN LA IS A MICROCOSM of the city's past, present, and future and one of its most intriguing neighborhoods. El Pueblo commemorates the city's Spanish origins, while Chinatown to the north and Little Tokyo to the south are the vibrant centers of immigrant communities. The city's financial pulse beats in glass high-rises along Flower and Figueroa Streets in sharp contrast to the eclectic early 20th-century architecture in the area around Pershing Square. Culture is king in downtown, from the renowned Museum of Contemporary Art and the spectacular new Walt Disney Concert Hall to the experimental galleries and studios of the Arts District east of Alameda Avenue. The Fashion and Jewelry Districts also add their own flair to the urban tapestry. Downtown is eminently walkable, but DASH buses also whisk you around between the diverse worlds that make up LA.

Restaurant in Chinatown

Downtown Sights

1. El Pueblo de Los Angeles
2. Union Station
3. Chinatown
4. Little Tokyo
5. City Hall
6. Cathedral of Our Lady of the Angels
7. Walt Disney Concert Hall
8. Museum of Contemporary Art (MOCA)
9. Bradbury Building
10. Grand Central Market

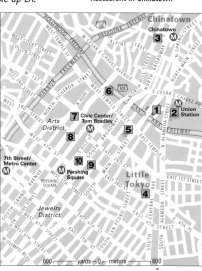

Union Station

El Pueblo de Los Angeles

1 This historic district near LA's 1781 founding site comprises buildings dating back to the early 19th century, when the city was little more than a scruffy outpost under Mexican rule. Its main artery, Olvera Street, has been restored to a lively lane lined with Mexican trinket shops and restaurants *(see pp20–1)*.

Union Station

2 Built in 1939 during the golden age of railroad travel, the design of the dignified Union Station blends traditional Spanish Mission elements with Modernist Art Deco touches. Its lofty main waiting room is graced with a coffered wooden ceiling, highly polished marble floors, and tall arched windows. Union Station has been featured in several movies, *The Hustler* (1961) and *Bugsy* (1992) among others. ◈ *Map X4 • 800 N Alameda St*

Chinatown

3 The Chinese first settled in LA after the Gold Rush, but were forced by the construction of Union Station to relocate a few blocks north to an area that is today known as "New Chinatown." The cultural hub of over 200,000 Chinese Americans, this exotic district has stores hawking dried and pickled ginger and lucky bamboo, the offices of herbalists and acupuncturists, and restaurants that serve hot dim sum. In February, the Chinese New Year is celebrated with colorful parades and dragon dances. ◈ *Map W2 • Along Broadway Hill north of Cesar Chavez Blvd*

Little Tokyo

4 The Japanese have been a presence in LA since the 1880s, but radical redevelopment in the 1960s replaced most of Little Tokyo's original structures with bland modern architecture. The few surviving buildings on East First Street are now protected as a National Historic Landmark. Stop at the Japanese American National Museum *(see p76)*, and check out the MOCA Geffen Contemporary *(see p76)* close by, and the Japanese Village Plaza. ◈ *Map W5 • Bounded by 1st & 4th, Alameda & Los Angeles Sts*

Japanese American National Museum

Chung King Road Galleries

This quiet, lantern-festooned lane in western Chinatown is the hotbed of LA's art scene. Artists' studios and no fewer than eight galleries have opened in between the traditional Chinese antique and furniture stores in the area. Follow a browsing session with a quiet drink at the venerable Hop Louie restaurant.

5 City Hall

LA's tallest building for over four decades, the central tower of this 1928 shiny white downtown presence was three times higher than the then height limit. A recent renovation has made it possible for the public to admire its marble-columned rotunda once again. City Hall has been immortalized on celluloid countless times, most famously as the headquarters of the *Daily Planet* in the *Superman* TV series. It was also attacked by Martians in *The War of the Worlds* (1954). ⊗ *Map W4* • *200 N Spring St* • *Open 8am–5pm Mon–Fri* • *Guided tours: 9am–2pm* • *Free*

6 Cathedral of Our Lady of the Angels

LA's strikingly modern Roman Catholic cathedral looms above the Hollywood Freeway that has been likened to a "river of transportation." Opened in 2002, the adobe-colored structure is entered through giant bronze

Rotunda in City Hall

doors cast by LA sculptor Robert Graham and guarded by a statue of Our Lady of the Angels. The soaring hall of worship, which seats 3,000 people, is bathed in soft light streaming in through alabaster windows. It is the first Catholic cathedral to be constructed in the western US in over a quarter century. ⊗ *Map V3* • *550 W Temple St* • *213-680-5200* • *Open 6:30am–6pm Mon–Fri, 9am–6pm Sat, 7am–6pm Sun* • *Free tours: 1pm Mon–Fri* • *www.olacathedral.org*

7 Walt Disney Concert Hall

The new home of the Los Angeles Philharmonic Orchestra (directed by Esa Pekka Salonen since 1991) is a spectacular addition to downtown's physical and cultural landscape. Frank Gehry conceived the dramatic design of this 2,265-seat auditorium, rather like the sculptural interpretation of a ship caught at sea. The exterior "sails" are clad in shining stainless steel panels, while the concert space itself boasts a curved wooden ceiling carefully calibrated for superb acoustics. ⊗ *Map V4* • *111 S Grand Ave* • *323-850-2000* • *www.laphil.com*

8 Museum of Contemporary Art (MOCA)

An early player in downtown's cultural renaissance, MOCA collects and displays art in all media from 1940 to the present. Works by Jackson Pollock, Andy Warhol, and Roy Lichtenstein form part of its permanent collection. The museum building, designed by famous Japanese architect Arata Isozaki, is a jumble of cubes, pyramids, and other shapes in reddish stone. ⊗ *Map U4* • *250 S Grand Ave* • *213-626-6222* • *Open 11am–5pm Mon–Fri (until 8pm Thu), 11am–6pm Sat & Sun* • *Adm (free on Thu)* • *www.moca-la.org*

Note: MOCA tickets are good for same-day entry at MOCA Geffen Contemporary and within 30 days at MOCA (Pacific Design Center)

Grand Central Market

9 Bradbury Building

The nondescript façade of this Victorian-era office building doesn't do justice to the magical courtyard within. Muted light filters in through a soaring glass roof while open-cage elevators take you up floors hemmed in by lacy banisters. Commissioned by the mining and real estate magnate Lewis Bradbury and completed in 1893, architect George Wyman allegedly found inspiration for some of his designs in Edward Bellamy's 1887 novel, *Looking Backward*. ✪ *Map V5 • 304 S Broadway • 213-687-0966 • Open 9am–5pm daily • Free*

10 Grand Central Market

Angelenos have perused the produce aisles of this exotic and lively market since 1917. Today, homemakers mingle with office workers to stock up on everything from fruits and vegetables to fresh fish and meat, and spices and herbs to cakes and bread, all available at bargain prices. Many of the eateries here also have long traditions, such as Roast-to-Go where the Penilla family has served made-to-order tacos and burritos since the 1950s. The architect Frank Lloyd Wright once had an office upstairs in this 1905 Beaux-Arts building. ✪ *Map V5 • 317 S Broadway • 213-624-2378 • Open 9am–6pm daily • www.grandcentralsquare.com*

A Day in Downtown

Morning

Begin your day with the historic **El Pueblo**, which will take you back to the city's vibrant Mexican and Spanish past. Browse colorful **Olvera Street** for authentic crafts and food, and then cross Alameda Street for a close-up of the grand **Union Station**.

Next, go west along Cesar Chavez Boulevard, before turning right on Broadway for a stroll through exotic **Chinatown** and a superb dim sum lunch at the **Empress Pavilion** (see p79).

Afternoon

Ride the DASH bus "B" from Broadway to Temple Street, dominated by the new **Cathedral of Our Lady of the Angels**. After admiring Rafael Moneo's Modernist masterpiece, head south along Grand Avenue, past the **Music Center** (see p54) and the **Walt Disney Concert Hall** to check out the latest exhibits at the **MOCA**.

Stroll down **Bunker Hill Steps** (see p77), stopping to gaze at "Source Figure," Robert Graham's exquisite sculpture and the **Central Library** (see p76). Walk to **Pershing Square** (see p76), lorded over by the baronial **Millennium Biltmore** (see p77), a nice place for tea or coffee. Leave in time to make it to the Victorian **Bradbury Building** before 5pm. Browse for treasures in the bountiful aisles of the **Grand Central Market**.

To get back to El Pueblo, board DASH bus "D" on Spring Street, changing to "B" at Temple Street.

 Following pages **Olvera Street marketplace**

Left **Central Library** Right **Pershing Square**

🔟 Best of the Rest

1 Wells Fargo History Museum

This little museum relives the days of the Wild West and houses an original stagecoach and a gold nugget from the Gold Rush. ◎ *Map U4 • 333 S Grand Ave • Open 9am–5pm Mon–Fri • Free*

2 Central Library

LA's main library consists of the original 1926 building, an exotic Beaux-Arts design by Bertram Goodhue, and an art-filled atrium added in 1993. ◎ *Map U5 • 630 W 5th St • 213-228-7000 • Open 10am–8pm Mon–Thu, 10am–6pm Fri & Sat, 1–5pm Sun*

3 Pershing Square

The city's oldest public park, redesigned in the early 1990s, it is enlivened with public art and flanked by numerous historic buildings, most notably the grand Biltmore. ◎ *Map U5*

4 Jewelry District

Precious gems, watches, and all kinds of fine jewelry are sold in shops in what has long been the center of Los Angeles's jewelry industry. ◎ *Map U5 • Hill St just off Pershing Square*

5 Fashion District

This 56-block district is the heart of LA's clothing industry (the largest in the nation) and heaven on earth for bargain hunters *(see p53)*. ◎ *Map U6 • Bounded by Broadway, San Pedro St, 7th St, & 16th St*

6 Flower Market

This 1913 cut-flower market, the largest in the country, has it all from roses to orchids. ◎ *Map V6 • 766 Wall St • 213-627-3696 • Open 8am–noon Mon, Wed, Fri, 6–11am Tue & Thu, 6am–noon Sat • Adm*

7 Museum of Neon Art (MONA)

The world's only permanent museum of its kind, MONA attracts visitors to its changing exhibitions of electric and neon art. ◎ *Map T6 • 501 W Olympic Blvd • 213-489-9918 • Open 11am–5pm Wed–Sat, noon–5pm Sun • Adm • www.neonmona.org*

8 Japanese American National Museum

Housed in a Buddhist temple, this museum chronicles the history of Japanese Americans. ◎ *Map W5 • 100 N Central Ave • 213-625-0414 • Open 10am–5pm Tue–Sun (until 8pm Thu) • Adm • www.janm.org*

9 MOCA Geffen Contemporary

This warehouse-sized former police garage hosts traveling shows and special exhibits *(see p71)*. ◎ *Map W5 • 152 N Central Ave • 213-626-6222 • Open 11am–5pm Mon–Fri (until 8pm Thu), 11am–6pm Sat & Sun • Adm*

10 Downtown Arts District

As artists move into studios here, hip galleries, shops, and restaurants have opened. ◎ *Map U4 • Bounded by 1st & 7th Sts, Alameda Ave, & the Los Angeles River*

  The Whole Foods Market at 239 North Crescent Drive has an enormous array of health food

Left **Westin Bonaventure** Center **Millennium Biltmore** Right **Eastern Columbia Building**

🔟 Downtown Architecture

1 Oviatt Building
This 1927 Art Deco gem features French fixtures and a forecourt adorned with Lalique glass. It houses the popular Cicada restaurant *(see p79)*.
🚇 Map U5 • 617 S Olive St

2 US Bank Tower
Shooting upward for about 1,017 ft (305 m), the tallest building between Chicago and Hong Kong was erected only after developers were forced to purchase the air rights from neighboring Central Library in order to exceed official height limits. 🚇 Map U5 • 633 W 5th St

3 Westin Bonaventure Hotel
The five mirror-glass cylinders of LA's biggest hotel look like a giant space ship ready for take-off *(see p150)*. 🚇 Map U4 • 404 S Figueroa Ave • 213-624-1000

4 Old Bank District
This trio of statuesque buildings, built between 1904 and 1910, have recently been converted into upscale lofts.
🚇 Map V5 • On 4th St between Main & Spring Sts

5 Millennium Biltmore
This palatial 1923 Beaux-Arts extravaganza includes architectural styles ranging from Renaissance to Neo-Classical *(see p144)*.

6 Fine Arts Building
Behind the richly detailed façade of this 1927 building awaits an amazing galleried lobby in Spanish Renaissance style.
🚇 Map T5 • 811 W 7th St Lobby • Open during office hours

7 Bunker Hill Steps
Cascading down from Hope Street to Fifth Street, these steps have many attractive features, including an amazing sculpture of a female nude by Robert Graham *(see p78)*. 🚇 Map U4

8 Eastern Columbia Building
This former furniture and clothing store from 1930 stands out for its bright turquoise terra-cotta mantle decorated with patterns. 🚇 Map U6 • 849 Broadway

9 Coca-Cola Bottling Plant
This Streamline Moderne building, located in an industrial area, resembles an ocean liner, complete with porthole windows. Two giant Coke bottles guard the corners. 🚇 Map E3 • 1334 S Central Ave • Not open to public

🔟 Broadway Historic Theater District
During the silent film era, Broadway was *the* movie district. The façades of the movie palaces are marvels of the imagination. 🚇 Map U6 • Along Broadway between 3rd & 9th Sts

Left **"Peace on Earth" by Jacques Lipchitz** Center & Right *Traveler* by Terry Schoonhoven

TOP10 Public Art

1 Peace on Earth
Created at the height of the Vietnam War in 1969, Jacques Lipchitz's large bronze Madonna has the dove, a symbol of peace, on top, and lambs, representing humanity, at the base. 🅜 *Map V4 • Music Center Plaza, 135 N Grand Ave*

2 Four Arches
Alexander Calder is best known for his mobiles, but this looming 1975 steel work painted in glowing fiery orange-red is a "stabile," an abstract stationary sculpture. 🅜 *Map U4 • 333 S Hope St*

3 Wells Fargo Court
The ground floor of this office complex is a treasure trove of public art with nudes by Robert Graham, Joan Miró's childlike *La Caresse d'un Oiseau*, and Jean Dubuffet's cartoonish *Le Dandy*. 🅜 *Map U4 • Wells Fargo Center, 333 S Grand Ave*

4 Source Figure
This bronze African-American female nude overlooks the Bunker Hill Steps *(see p77)*. Designed by Robert Graham in 1992, she represents the source of the water cascading down the stairs. 🅜 *Map U4 • Hope St, near 4th St*

5 Corporate Head
This evocative sculpture (1990) by Terry Allen and Philip Levine condemns the greed and erosion of moral responsibility in today's corporate America. 🅜 *Map T5 • 725 S Figueroa St*

6 Spine
This 1993 installation by Jud Fine is a visual allegory of a book – the well symbolizes the title page, the step risers the pages, and the pools the plot flow. 🅜 *Map U4 • Maguire Gardens, northern side of Central Library, Flower, & 5th Sts*

7 Biddy Mason: A Passage of Time
This memorial by Betye Saar and Sheila de Bretteville commemorates the story of former slave, Biddy Mason (1818–91), a leader who established the city's first black church. 🅜 *Map V5 • 333 S Spring St, near 3rd St*

8 Astronaut Ellison S. Onizuka Memorial
A 1/10th scale model of the *Challenger*, this 1990 memorial by Isao Hirai honors the first Japanese-American astronaut. 🅜 *Map W5 • Onizuka St, Little Tokyo*

9 Molecule Man
This monumental 1991 sculpture by Jonathan Borofsky shows four embracing figures, symbolizing the commonality between people based on their shared molecular structure. 🅜 *Map W4 • 255 E Temple St*

10 Traveler
Terry Schoonhoven's 1993 ceramic mural depicts California travelers from the days of the Spanish explorations, and LA landmarks such as Pico House *(see p21)*. 🅜 *Map X4 • Union Station*

Ciudad

Price Categories

Price categories include a three-course meal for one, a glass of house wine, and all unavoidable extra charges including tax.

$ under $25
$$ $25–$50
$$$ $50–$80
$$$$ over $80

🔟 Places to Eat

1 Water Grill
Fish and seafood fanciers from all over flock to this clubby shrine, which uses only impeccably fresh ingredients. Desserts are superb. ✎ *Map U5 • 544 S Grand Ave • 213-891-0900 • $$$*

2 Cicada
The sumptuous Art Deco dining room in the historic Oviatt Building almost overshadows the food. The Northern Italian menu features classics. ✎ *Map U5 • 617 S Olive St • 213-488-9488 • $*

3 Ciudad
The urban jazzy pan-Latino decor here is as bold and exuberant as the food created by star chefs Mary Sue Milliken and Susan Feniger. ✎ *Map U4 • 445 S Figueroa St • 213-486-5171 • $$*

4 Nick & Stef's Steakhouse
Loosen your belt for the juiciest steaks ever. Preview your cut in the glass-encased aging chamber. ✎ *Map U4 • 330 S Hope St, Wells Fargo Center • 213-680-0330 • $*

5 McCormick & Schmick's
This vast wood and leather seafood restaurant has the city's finest Happy Hours with fish tacos, stir-fried rice, and other fun fare at bargain prices.
✎ *Map U4 • 633 W 5th St • 213-629-1929 • $$*

6 Philippe the Original
This "original" hasn't gone out of fashion since it first began serving bulging French-dipped meat sandwiches in 1908. ✎ *Map X2 • 1001 N Alameda St • 213-628-3781 • No credit cards • Veg: salads only • $*

7 Empress Pavilion
For great dim sum, snag a table in this Chinatown banquet hall. Try the bite-sized stuffed wontons and short ribs. ✎ *Map W2 • 988 N Hill St, Bamboo Plaza • 213-617-9898 • $*

8 Yang Chow
In this reliable Chinese eatery, a plate of the hallmark "slippery shrimp" graces almost every table. The *moo-shu* pork is also a good bet. ✎ *Map W2 • 819 N Broadway, Chinatown • 213-625-0811 • $*

9 R-23
Canvases adorn the walls of this sophisticated sushi parlor in a former warehouse in the Arts District. The raw fish morsels are divine. ✎ *Map X5 • 923 E 2nd St • 213-687-7178 • Closed Sun • $$$*

10 Angelique Café
Great French country cooking at pauper-friendly prices are the hallmark of this Fashion District favorite which serves great paté. ✎ *Map U6 • 840 S Spring St • 213-623-8698 • Breakfast & lunch only • Closed Sun • $*

Left **Dodger Stadium** Center **California African American Museum** Right **Southwest Museum**

Around Downtown

I T HAS BEEN SAID THAT LA IS NOT *really a city, but a collection of 88 independent towns that overlap. Nowhere is this truer than within the 5-mile (8-km) radius of the center of downtown. West of here, Koreatown is home to the largest Korean population in the US, while east LA has the largest group of Latinos living outside Latin America. In the Latino-Byzantine quarter, surrounding the Greek Orthodox St. Sophia Cathedral on Normandie*

Avenue, Latinos and Greeks predominate and complement each other. Northeast of downtown is Dodger Stadium, a world-famous landmark, while south of the center lies Exposition Park with its museums and sports venues. This area constitutes a melting pot for people belonging to different races and geographical regions. America needs no better mirror than the city of Los Angeles to see what it will one day surely become.

Natural History Museum

🔟 Sights

1. **Natural History Museum**
2. **California African American Museum**
3. **California Science Center**
4. **Dodger Stadium**
5. **Angelino Heights**
6. **Heritage Square Museum**
7. **Lummis House**
8. **Southwest Museum**
9. **St. Sophia Cathedral**
10. **San Antonio Winery**

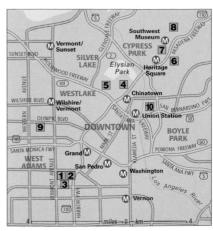

1 Natural History Museum

It's easy to spend a day exploring this engaging museum, the nation's second largest of its kind. The dinosaurs always draw huge crowds, as do the dioramas of African and North American mammals, and the grisly 14.5-ft (4-m) long megamouth, the rarest shark in the world. The Gem and Mineral Hall contains a huge gold exhibit and a dazzling walk-through gem vault. Cultural exhibits explain and highlight the traditions of Native and Latin American civilizations. Children love the hands-on activities in the Discovery Center and the Insect Zoo. ⊗ *Map D3 • 900 Exposition Blvd, Exposition Park • 213-763-3466 • Open 9:30am–5pm Mon–Fri, 10am–5pm Sat–Sun • Adm (free for under 5s) • www.nhm.org*

2 California African American Museum

This recently renovated museum celebrates the art, history, and culture of African Americans, especially in relation to California and the western US. The main exhibit traces the journey from Africa to slavery in the American South to final freedom on the West Coast. It includes memorabilia donated by singer Ella Fitzgerald and former LA mayor Tom Bradley. Temporary shows highlight particular artists, including emerging ones. ⊗ *Map D3 • 600 State Dr, Exposition Park • 213-744-7432 • Open 10am–4pm Wed–Sat • Free • www.caam.ca.gov*

3 California Science Center

Filled with clever and engaging interactive exhibits, this highly entertaining science and technology museum has three themed galleries. The World of Life exhibit explains the processes living organisms undergo, Creative World focuses on the ability of humans to adapt to their environment through technology, and the Air and Space Gallery explores the great beyond. But it's a 50-ft (15-m) long animatronic doll stripped down to her organs that steals the show and attracts crowds. ⊗ *Map D3 • 700 State Drive, Exposition Park • 323-724-3623 • Open 10am–5pm • Free • www.cascisencectr.org*

4 Dodger Stadium

For many, spring wouldn't be the same without baseball. The pilgrimage to Dodger Stadium to watch the "Boys in Blue" fight it out is an annual ritual for thousands of fans. Hunkered in the bleachers, munching on the famous Dodger Dogs, they watch their team (LA Dodgers) in action. The stadium opened in 1962 and is often called one of USA's most beautiful ballparks. It has hosted eight World Series, many concerts, and even a papal mass. ⊗ *Map W1 • 1000 Elysian Park Ave • 323-224-1448 • Tours (on non-game days by appointment only), tickets required • www.dodgers.com*

California Science Center

Koreatown
Parts of western Vermont Avenue around Wilshire Boulevard west of downtown would not look out of place in Seoul. They are the main arteries of Koreatown, which is home to the largest Korean population in the US and a beehive of commercial activity. Learn more about the Korean community at the Korean Cultural Center at 5505 Wilshire Blvd.

Angelino Heights
In the 1880s, this was one of LA's first suburbs and an elegant neighborhood with stately Victorian mansions along streets such as Carroll Avenue and Kellam Avenue. Many surviving buildings have been lovingly restored by their current owners. The 1300 block of Carroll Avenue has the finest, including the Haskin House at No. 1344 and the Foy House at No. 1325. They are open to the public only during tours run by the LA Conservancy *(see p138)*. ✪ Map U1 • Carroll Ave & Kellam Ave, Echo Park

Heritage Square Museum
Unlike those on Carroll Avenue, most other Victorian-era homes had a date with the wrecking ball. A few were spared destruction and were air-lifted by helicopter to form the Heritage Square Museum. Eight vintage beauties cluster here – five residences, a church, a barn, and a railroad depot that also happens to be a visitor center, all sporting gables and turrets. The Hale House, impressively restored, stands out from the rest. ✪ Map E2 • 3800 Homer St, Highland Park • 626-449-0193 • Open seasonal hours • Adm • www.heritagesquare.org

Lummis House
Now the headquarters of the Historical Society of Southern California, this was once the home of the eccentric Charles Fletcher Lummis (1859–1928), who walked the entire 3,000 miles (4,830 km) from Ohio to LA in 1885. Best known as an outspoken California booster and preservationist, Lummis built his house with his own hands out of concrete and found materials, including boulders and railroad rails. The house is also known as El Alisal, the Spanish name for sycamore, which once grew here in abundance. ✪ Map E2 • 200 E Ave 43, Highland Park • 323-222-0546 • Open noon–4pm Fri–Sun • Donation

Lummis House

Southwest Museum
The oldest museum in Los Angeles was the brainchild of Charles Lummis, whose personal collection of Native American artifacts formed the basis of its holdings. It has one of the nation's largest and most important collections of Native art and artifacts. Galleries provide a survey of the traditions of Native cultures from California, the Great Plains, the

Hale House, Heritage Square Museum

Southwest, and the Pacific Northwest. A famous collection of baskets are intriguing exhibits. 🗺 Map E2 • 234 Museum Dr, Highland Park • 323-221-2164 • Open 10am–5pm Tue–Sun • Adm • www.southwestmuseum.org

A Sequoyah Indian relief, Southwest Museum

9 St. Sophia Cathedral

One of LA's surprises, St. Sophia, the central church of Southern California's Greek community, was masterminded by the Skouras brothers, a trio of movie impresarios. Behind its austere, gleaming white exterior is an exceptionally opulent hall of worship. The eye is drawn to the icon-studded, golden altar of the Virgin Mary while Jesus, surrounded by saints, looks down at the congregation from the 90-ft (27-m) high dome. 🗺 Map D3 • 1324 S Normandie Ave, Koreatown • 323-737-2424 • Open 10am–4pm Tue–Fri, 10am–2pm Sat • Free • www.stsophia.org

10 San Antonio Winery

LA's only surviving winery is tucked away in the industrial area north of the Los Angeles River. It's hard to imagine that this bleak area was once blanketed with vineyards. When the founder of San Antonio, Santo Cambianica, arrived in 1917, he faced stiff competition from over 100 wineries. Prohibition put most out of business, but Santo survived making sacramental wine. Even today, fermentation continues to take place here. Taste the wines; the restaurant is a popular lunch spot (see p85). 🗺 Map E2 • 737 Lamar St, Lincoln Heights, 323-223-1401, www.sanantonio winery.com • Tasting room open 8:30am–7pm Wed–Fri, 8:30am–6pm Mon & Tue, 9am–7pm Sat, 10am–6pm Sun • Free

Exploring Exposition Park in a Day

Morning

Start at **Exposition Park** from Figueroa Street and make the **Natural History Museum** the first stop of the day. Admire its lovely façade, before delving into the exhibits inside. A landmark bronze sculpture of a *Tyrannosaurus rex* battling a Triceratops stands to the north outside. Crossing the street takes you to the **University of Southern California** campus (see p84), where you can join a free guided tour offered hourly from 10am to 3pm. Have lunch on campus or walk east on Exposition Boulevard to the **Mercado La Paloma**, a Latin-flavored community center with colorful crafts stalls and casual eating joints.

Afternoon

Backtrack to Exposition Park and start the afternoon with a look at the **Los Angeles Memorial Coliseum** (see p47), the main venue of the 1932 and 1984 Olympics. The two huge headless bronze figures outside the eastern entrance were designed by local sculptor Robert Graham. Just north of here is the **California Science Center**, with many interactive exhibits. Grab a cold drink from the downstairs cafeteria and head outside to the fragrant **Rose Garden** (see p42) to relax. If you still have the energy left, do check out the latest exhibits at the **California African American Museum**. Otherwise, wind down the day with a 3D visual adventure at the **IMAX Theater** (see p57) next to the Science Center.

Left **Shrine Auditorium** Right **Boots at El Mercado**

Best of the Rest

1 Angelus Temple
Founded by a popular preacher with a flair for theatrics, this 1923 domed building was once the headquarters of the Foursquare Gospel Church.
◈ *Map E1 • 1100 Glendale Blvd, Echo Park • Open only during special events*

2 The Wiltern
This live concert venue is encased by the lovely 1931 Art Deco Pelissier Building. ◈ *Map D2 • 3790 Wilshire Blvd, Koreatown*

3 Bullocks Wilshire Building
One of the earliest Art Deco structures in the country, this beautiful building now houses the Southwestern University School of Law. ◈ *Map D2 • 3050 Wilshire Blvd, Koreatown*

4 Shrine Auditorium
This 1926 Moorish-style theater seats up to 6,700 and was once the largest in the United States. ◈ *Map D3 • 665 W Jefferson Blvd, Exposition Park area*

5 University of Southern California (USC)
Built in 1880, the oldest private university in Western US counts George Lucas in its alumni. ◈ *Map D3 • Bounded by Jefferson, Figueroa, Exposition Blvds, & Vermont Ave, Exposition Park area • 213-740-2311 • www.usc.edu*

6 William Andrews Clark Memorial Library
This 1926 building has a rare collection of English books only available to scholars, and an oak-paneled music room. ◈ *Map D3 • 2520 Cimarron St, W Adams district • 323-735-7605 • Tours by appointment*

7 El Mercado
This indoor marketplace offers a peek into Mexican-American culture. Stop for an authentic meal or browse colorful stalls. ◈ *Map E3 • 3425 E 1st St, E LA • 323-268-3451 • Open 10am–8pm Mon–Fri, 9am–9pm Sat & Sun*

8 Self-help Graphics & Arts
This nonprofit arts center works chiefly with the Latino community. Visit the Galeria Otra Vez. ◈ *Map E3 • 3802 Cesar E Chavez Ave, E LA • 323-881-6444 • Gallery hours: 10am–4pm Tue–Sat, noon–4pm Sun • Free*

9 Mariachi Plaza
Mariachi musicians in black robes gather in this small park, waiting to be hired for the night's engagements. ◈ *Map E2 • Corner of Boyle Ave & 1st St, E LA*

10 Brewery Arts Complex
This massive artist colony organizes art walks twice yearly. ◈ *Map E2 • 2100 N Main St, Lincoln Heights • 213-694-2911 • Gallery open Fri–Sun (by appointment) • Free*

Guelaguetza

Price Categories

Price categories include a three-course meal for one, a glass of house wine, and all unavoidable extra charges including tax.

$	under $25
$$	$25–$50
$$$	$50–$80
$$$$	over $80

Places to Eat

1 Maddalena Restaurant
This slice of Italy, ensconced in what was once the fermentation cellars of the San Antonio Winery, is a popular lunch spot. ⊗ Map E2 • 737 Lamar St, Lincoln Heights • 323-223-1401 • Lunch only • $

2 La Serenata de Garibaldi
The original branch of a small chain of upscale Mexican restaurants, it serves fish and seafood in divinely flavored sauces. ⊗ Map E2 • 1842 E 1st St, Boyle Heights • 323-265-2887 • $$

3 El Tepeyac
Lines form outside LA's burrito "headquarters" for the bulging "Hollenbeck," stuffed with guacamole and pork. ⊗ Map E2 • 812 N Evergreen Ave, E LA • 323-267-8668 • No credit cards • $

4 Barbara's at the Brewery
This self-service bistro in the Brewery Arts Complex doubles as an art gallery, with changing displays of work. ⊗ Map E2 • 620 Moulton Ave, Suite 110, Lincoln Heights • 323-221-9204 • No dis. access • $

5 Soot Bull Jeep
Grill your own deliciously marinated meat over charcoal at this authentic Korean barbecue place. ⊗ Map D2 • 3136 8th St, Koreatown • 213-387-3865 • $

6 Guelaguetza
This lively restaurant serving food from southern Mexico is famous for its *moles* – sauces made from spices, nuts, chilies, and chocolate. ⊗ Map D2 • 3337 1/2 W 8th St, Koreatown • 213-427-0601 • $$

7 Papa Christo's Taverna
Drop into this friendly, busy eatery next door to St. Sophia *(see p83)* for fat portions of great Greek food. ⊗ Map D3 • 2771 W Pico Blvd, Koreatown • 323-737-2970 • $

8 El Cholo
This festive Mexican eatery has been full of diners hungry for fajitas and burritos since 1923. Their margaritas pack a wicked punch. ⊗ Map D3 • 1121 S Western Ave, Koreatown • 323-734-2773 • $

9 Taylor's Steakhouse
Send your cholesterol count through the roof at this venerable throwback to the 1950s, with faux leather booths and yummy steaks almost the size of baseball mitts. ⊗ Map D2 • 3361 W 8th St, Koreatown • 213-382-8449 • $$

10 Taix
This 1927 eatery serves value portions of country classics such as delicious roast chicken with *bordelaise* sauce. Great soups. ⊗ Map E2 • 1911 Sunset Blvd, Echo Park • 213-484-1265 • $

Unless otherwise stated, all restaurants accept credit cards, serve vegetarian meals, and provide access for the disabled

85

Left **Castle Green, Old Pasadena** Right **The Pasadena Museum of California Art sign**

Pasadena

PASADENA MAY BE CONSIDERED PART OF LA, *but is, in fact, distinctly apart.* As LA's first suburb, it attracted a large share of the rich and the powerful who saw to it that a European flair enhanced the town. Fine mansions, such as the masterful Craftsman-era Gamble House, occupy grounds on leafy streets. Old Town Pasadena, the historic core, has been renovated to create a vibrant street with fine restaurants and shops. Pasadena is in the limelight every year on January 1 with its Tournament of Roses, a parade and football game. The area's other treasures include the Rose Bowl and the fabled Huntington Gardens.

Wrigley Mansion & Garden

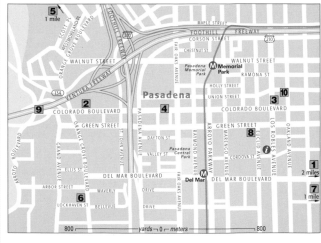

Stop by the Pasadena Visitors Center located at 171 South Los Robles Avenue

Still Life with Lemons, Oranges, & a Rose by Zurbarán, Norton Simon Museum

1 Huntington Library, Art Collections, & Botanical Gardens

This treasure trove of high culture is the legacy of railroad baron Henry E. Huntington. He made his vast fortune as a real estate speculator and owner of LA's first mass transit system, the Big Red Cars *(see p25)*.

2 Norton Simon Museum

This must-see for art lovers owes its existence to Norton Simon, a hugely successful entrepreneur who amassed hundreds of masterpieces *(see p90)* from the Renaissance to the 20th century, and sculpture from India and Southeast Asia. Old Masters such as Rembrandt and Goya and the Impressionists, especially Degas, as well as Renoir, Cézanne, and Monet are well represented. Frank Gehry's recent remodel improved the lighting conditions of the exhibit space. Sculptures, including Rodin's *The Thinker*, dot the gardens, inspired by Monet's at Giverny in France. ◈ *Map E1 • 411 W Colorado Blvd • 626-449-6840 • Open noon–6pm Wed–Mon, until 9pm Fri • Adm (free for under 19s and students with ID) • www.nortonsimon.org*

3 Pacific Asia Museum

Grace Nicholson, infatuated with all things Asian, had her 1920s private home designed to look like a Chinese imperial palace. It now makes a fitting setting for this museum's artifacts from Asia and the Pacific Islands. Exhibits, usually drawn from the 14,000-strong collection, feature masks from New Guinea, paintings by Japanese masters Hokusai and Hiroshige, and woven costumes from Pakistan. ◈ *Map F1 • 46 N Los Robles Ave • 626-449-2742 • Open 10am–5pm Wed–Sun, until 8pm Fri • Adm • www.pacificasiamuseum.org*

4 Old Town Pasadena

Pasadena's historic business district along western Colorado Boulevard was once a decaying part of town, but has now been restored. Today, its handsome brick buildings are packed with boutiques, restaurants, and bookstores. A short detour will take you to the imposing 1898 Castle Green, an apartment building that was once Old Pasadena's most luxurious resort hotel. ◈ *Map F1 • Along Colorado Blvd between Marengo Ave & Pasadena Ave • Castle Green, 50 E Green St*

For more on the Huntington Library, Art Collections, & Botanical Gardens **See pp22–5**

Doo Dah Parade

This over-the-top celebration of wackiness, held every June, began in 1978 as an irreverent spoof of the wholesome Rose Parade. Entrants vary each year but groups such as the Synchronized Precision Briefcase Drill Team and the West Hollywood Transvestite Cheerleaders always generate cheers from the 40,000-strong crowd on Colorado Boulevard.

5 Rose Bowl

Pasadena's most famous landmark, the Rose Bowl draws worldwide attention every New Year's Day when two top-ranking college football teams battle it out for the Rose Bowl Game Trophy. College football first became part of the Tournament of Roses in 1902 when Stanford was trounced 49-0 by Michigan. Architect Myron Hunt's originally horseshoe-shaped structure was later converted into an elliptical shape and enlarged to its current seating capacity of 93,000. ✆ *Map E1 • 1001 Rose Bowl Dr • 626-577-3100 • www.rosebowlstadium.com*

6 Wrigley Mansion & Garden

William Wrigley Jr, the man who gave the world Wrigley's chewing gum, certainly knew how to live. His winter residence in Pasadena is an 18,500-sq-ft (1,720-sq-m) Renaissance-style mansion. It houses the Tournament of Roses Association, which organizes the annual New Year's Day Rose Parade and the Rose Bowl Game. Memorabilia includes Rose Queen crowns, trophies, and photographs. ✆ *Map E1 • 391 S Orange Grove Blvd • 626-449-4100 • Tours: 2–4pm Thu Feb–Aug • Free • www.tournamentofroses.com*

7 California Institute of Technology (CalTech)

One of the world's leading scientific research centers and a pioneer in earthquake science and molecular biology, CalTech counts 29 Nobel Prize winners among its alumni and faculty, including biologist and current president, David Baltimore. The institute evolved from an arts and crafts school founded in 1891 by the famous Amos G. Throop, changing its focus to science after astronomer George E. Hale became a board member in 1907. ✆ *Map F2 • 1200 E California Blvd • 626-395-6811 • Campus open anytime • Free guided tours: 2pm Mon–Fri (no tours during the winter break & on rainy days) • www.caltech.edu*

8 Pasadena Civic Center

This grand complex was inspired by the early 20th-century City Beautiful movement. It

Rose Bowl

City Hall, Pasadena Civic Center

consists of three European-style Beaux-Arts structures stretching along a central axis – the Main Library, the Civic Auditorium, and the City Hall. Architect Myron Hunt designed the public library. ◉ *Map F1 • City Hall, 100 N Garfield Ave, 626-744-4000 • Civic Auditorium, 300 E Green St, 626-449-7360 • Library, 285 E Walnut St, 626-744-4052*

9 Colorado Street Bridge

The graceful arches of this recently restored 1913 bridge straddle the Arroyo Seco (Spanish for "dry brook"), a natural ravine that comes down from the San Gabriel Mountains. The imposing 1903 Vista del Arroyo Hotel overlooking the bridge is presently home to the Ninth Circuit Court of Appeals. ◉ *Map E1 • Court • 125 S Grand Ave • Tours by appointment only • 626-229-7250*

10 Pasadena Museum of California Art

Pasadena art collectors, Robert and Arlene Oltman, occupy the third floor of their 2002 custom-built museum, the only one in the state solely devoted to the art and architecture of California. Watercolors, photographs, and the works of historical as well as living artists are showcased. ◉ *Map F1 • 490 E Union St • 626-568-3665 • Open noon–5pm Wed–Sun • Adm (free for under 12s) • www.pmcaonline.org*

Exploring Historic Pasadena

Morning

A classic way to start the day in Pasadena is with an energizing breakfast at **Marston's** *(see p93)*. After your fill of pancakes, stroll east a couple of blocks on Walnut Street and have a look at the beautiful Beaux-Arts **Main Library** and the majestic **City Hall** a little to the south. Continue farther south to Colorado Boulevard, then head west to **Old Pasadena**, the city's original downtown, a popular shopping and dining district. Check out the well-restored historic façades while browsing the stores, then pause briefly for a snack or perhaps a cold beer at the **Gordon Biersch Brewery Restaurant** *(see p93)*.

Afternoon

In the afternoon, either drive or walk west along Colorado Boulevard, then turn right on Orange Grove Boulevard to catch the 1pm or 2pm tour of the **Gamble House** *(see p91)*, the Craftsman-era magnum opus by Charles and Henry Greene. Fans of this architectural style could check out several more residences designed by the brothers along nearby Arroyo Terrace and Grand Avenue. Others can make their way back to Colorado Boulevard for a visit to the first-rate **Norton Simon Museum**. The gorgeous gardens are a nice place for a respite and refreshments. A perfect finale to your day is to treat yourself to a grand dinner at **The Raymond** *(see p93)*, one of the city's oldest and most popular restaurants.

Left **Norton Simon Museum** Center **Rembrandt's** *Self-Portrait* Right **Rousseau's** *Exotic Landscape*

TOP 10 Artworks at the Norton Simon Museum

1 Madonna & Child with a Book
Renaissance artist Raphael (1483–1520) was only 19 years old when he painted this work. It perfectly exemplifies his geometrically balanced compositions and ability to imbue his figures with spirituality and tenderness.

2 Self-Portrait
No artist has left behind such a thorough record of his own likeness as Rembrandt (1606–69). The elegant garb, dapper beret, and gold chain in this portrait emphasize his social status as a sought-after artist.

3 Still Life with Lemons, Oranges, & a Rose
In this still life, Francisco de Zurbarán (1598–1664) applies the bright colors and minute detail usually reserved for his depictions of saints and clergy.

4 The Triumph of Virtue & Nobility Over Ignorance
Rococo master Giovanni Battista Tiepolo (1696–1770) is known for his exuberant ceiling frescoes. This canvas shows off his bold compositions and use of color.

5 The Artist's Garden at Vétheuil
Claude Monet (1840–1926) looked out from his house on the Seine at the sunny, flower-filled garden of this painting.

6 The Little Fourteen-Year-Old Dancer
Edgar Degas (1834–1917) was fascinated with dancers, and this exquisite sculpture is one of his finest. The figure is partly painted, dressed in a tulle skirt, and has been given real hair.

7 Portrait of a Peasant
Vincent Van Gogh (1853–90) painted Patience Escalier, a gardener and shepherd, against a night-blue background to create "a mysterious effect, like a star in the depths of an azure sky."

8 Exotic Landscape
Henri Rousseau (1844–1910) is renowned for his poetic, naive paintings that depict magical, lushly landscaped dream worlds. He created this work shortly before his death.

9 Woman with a Book
A highlight of the museum's extensive Picasso (1881–1973) holdings, this graceful painting shows the artist's mistress, Marie-Therèse Walter, in an introspective mood that contrasts sharply with the melodramatic colors.

10 Shiva & Parvati
This pair of 11th-century Indian bronze sculpture casts depict the Hindu god Shiva, part of the holy Trinity of gods, accompanied by his wife Parvati.

The main floor of this museum showcases European art while the lower galleries display Indian and Southeast Asian art

Left **Tiffany lamp, Gamble House** Center **Charles Sumner Greene House** Right **Halsted House**

🔟 Greene & Greene Craftsman Houses

Around Town – Pasadena

1 The Gamble House (1908)
This handcrafted masterpiece *(see p40)* is a symphony of rich wood, leaded glass windows, and a stained-glass Tiffany door. ◈ *Map E1 • 4 Westmoreland Place • 626-793-3334 • Tours noon–3pm Thu–Sun • Adm (free for under 12s) • www.gamblehouse.org*

2 The Cole House (1906)
This large home, owned by a church, marks the first time the Greenes added a *porte-cochere* (a porchlike roof) above the driveway in front of the house. ◈ *Map E1 • 2 Westmoreland Place*

3 The Ranney House (1907)
Mary Ranney worked as a draftsperson at the brothers' firm and contributed many of the design ideas for this lovely shingled corner mansion. ◈ *Map E1 • 440 Arroyo Terrace*

4 The Hawks House (1906)
This home is distinguished by a very wide covered porch, which keeps out the heat as well as the light, giving the house a rather sombre appearance. ◈ *Map E1 • 408 Arroyo Terrace*

5 The Van Rossem-Neill House (1903)
Hemmed in by an unusual wall made of warped clinker bricks and boulders, this pretty house has a stained-glass front door. ◈ *Map E1 • 400 Arroyo Terrace*

6 The White Sisters House (1903)
This house has lost much of its Craftsman look thanks to the replacement of the shingle exterior with painted stucco. ◈ *Map E1 • 370 Arroyo Terrace*

7 The Charles Sumner Greene House (1901–16)
Charles experimented with many Craftsman ideas while building his own home. The front room, buttressed by boulders and bricks, was a later addition. ◈ *Map E1 • 368 Arroyo Terrace*

8 The Duncan-Irwin House (1902)
This large, beautiful home, originally a single story bungalow, pays homage to Japanese design with its slightly upturned roofs. ◈ *Map E1 • 240 N Grand Ave*

9 The James Culbertson House (1902–15)
The stained-glass entrance door, the clinker brick wall, and the pergola are the only surviving Greene & Greene elements of this extensively remodeled home. ◈ *Map E1 • 235 N Grand Ave*

10 The Halsted House (1905)
Originally one of the brothers' smallest designs, this bungalow sports a deep overhang of eaves sheltering the main entrance along the driveway side. ◈ *Map E1 • 90 N Grand Ave*

Unless otherwise stated, all the Craftsman Houses are closed to the public

Left **Shops in Old Pasadena** Right **The Illuminations sign**

TOP 10 Shopping in Old Pasadena

1 Sur La Table
Cooking aficionados love browsing through this vast assortment of quality kitchenware, from pots and pans to hard-to-find utensils. ✆ *161 W Colorado Blvd • 626-744-9987*

2 Restoration Hardware
This retro emporium specializes in reproductions of classic furniture and period hardware such as door knobs, but also has a fun selection of trendy home accessories. ✆ *127 W Colorado Blvd • 626-795-7234*

3 Shizu Japanese Paper & Origami
Besides exquisite handmade paper and origami supplies, this small but stylish store stocks an unusual line of Japanese gift items and artworks. ✆ *120 W Colorado Blvd • 626-395-7293*

4 Lather
This "modern apothecary" uses only natural ingredients for its innovative skin care products and has an assortment of olive oil soap sold by weight. ✆ *106 W Colorado Blvd • 877-652-8437*

5 Armani Exchange
The *prêt-a-porter* line by Italian fashion mogul Giorgio Armani is aimed at the client who loves fashionable clothes. It reflects his hallmark simplicity and sophisticated style, but at more affordable prices. ✆ *29 W Colorado Blvd • 626-795-7527*

6 Penny Lane
One of LA's few remaining independent music stores, this small outlet has used music CDs available very cheaply as well as vinyl albums, new music, and listening stations. ✆ *12 W Colorado Blvd • 626-564-0161*

7 J. Crew
The retail store of this famous catalog line has the same practical yet stylish clothing and accessories for men and women at reasonable prices. ✆ *3 W Colorado Blvd • 626-568-2739*

8 Canyon Beachwear
Swimsuits are the quintessential LA accessory, and this store stocks a large number, which range from figure flattering one-pieces to sexy, barely-there string bikinis. ✆ *34 Hugus Alley • 626-564-0752*

9 Illuminations
This small store spills over with candles of all kinds, from votives to pillars, scented to fragrance-free, and floating to jarred. It also stocks all kinds of fun and funky accessories. ✆ *15 E Colorado Blvd • 626-577-5113*

10 Sixty East Gallery
The ring is the thing to buy at this innovative jewelry studio and gallery whose vast collection also includes beautiful, cutting-edge steel and diamond bands to die for. ✆ *60 E Colorado Blvd • 626-683-2574 • Closed Sun & Mon*

Price Categories

Price categories include a three-course meal for one, a glass of house wine, and all unavoidable extra charges including tax.

$	under $25
$$	$25–$50
$$$	$50–$80
$$$$	over $80

Left **Parkway Grill** Center **Marston's** Right **Café Santorini**

Places to Eat

1 Saladang Song
Complex flavors and a lovely Post-Modern patio make this trendy Thai eatery a Pasadena favorite. Insiders swear by the delicious flavored rice soup breakfast. ◉ *Map F2 • 383 S Fair Oak Ave • 626-793-5200 • $*

2 Yujean Kang's
Items such as Ants on Tree (glass noodles with flank steak) and Chinese shrimp *polenta* are served in this unusual Chinese restaurant. The wine list is excellent. ◉ *Map F1 • 67 N Raymond Ave • 626-585-0855 • $$*

3 Marston's
Start the day with blueberry pancakes, golden French toast, or other breakfast favorites at this popular cottage hangout. ◉ *Map F1 • 151 E Walnut St • 626-796-2459 • Closed Mon • $*

4 The Raymond
One of Pasadena's finest restaurants, this Craftsman-style cottage has a menu of American classics. ◉ *Map F2 • 1250 S Fair Oaks Ave at Columbia St • 626-441-3136 • Veg: Limited • Closed Mon • $$$$*

5 Parkway Grill
Only the freshest organic ingredients are used to perfect inspired Californian cuisine. ◉ *Map F2 • 510 S Arroyo Parkway • 626-795-1001 • $$$*

6 Kuala Lumpur
This eatery provides a good introduction to Malaysian food. Try the *rojak*, a zesty salad, and the yummy coconut-based *laksa* curry. ◉ *Map F1 • 69 W Green St • 626-577-5175 • Closed Mon • $*

7 Bistro 45
This classy place in a beautifully restored Art Deco building turns out excellent French fare paired with one of the best wine lists in town. ◉ *Map F1 • 45 S Mentor Ave • 626-795-2478 • Veg: Limited • Closed Mon • $*

8 Café Santorini
The tables on the terrace are the most coveted on balmy summer evenings. The Greek and Italian menu has lots of fun appetizers. ◉ *Map F1 • 64 W Union St • 626-564-4200 • No dis. access • $*

9 Sushi Roku
Classic sushi and creative new takes on Asian food keep this attractively designed place busy. ◉ *Map F1 • 33 Miller Alley • 626-683-3000 • $$$*

10 Gordon Biersch Brewery Restaurant
Most people come here for the signature German-style brews, but the upscale beer hall fare is equally satisfying and filling. ◉ *Map F1 • 41 Hugus Alley • 626-449-0052 • $*

Unless otherwise stated, all restaurants accept credit cards, serve vegetarian meals, and provide access for the disabled

93

Left **Hollywood & Highland Complex** Right **Paramount Studios entrance**

Hollywood

HOLLYWOOD IS AT ONCE A TOWN, *an industry, and an illusion, and you'll experience all of these as you stroll along the famed Hollywood Boulevard. Its history encompasses the birth of the movies, the Golden Age of film premieres, and a crushing decline as the studios moved elsewhere. But recent years have seen a renaissance along the boulevard – the Hollywood and Highland complex is a major development, and many of the grand movie palaces once again host glamorous film openings. At its core, Hollywood is a museum – the huge sign in the hills, movie stars "at your feet" on the Walk of Fame, the bars that hosted greats such as Ernest Hemingway – this is still the place to rekindle childhood dreams about the "stars."*

🔟 Sights

1. Hollywood Boulevard
2. Hollywood Sign
3. Hollywood Bowl
4. Hollywood Heritage Museum
5. Hollywood Forever Cemetery
6. Paramount Studios
7. Cinerama Dome
8. Crossroads of the World
9. Silver Lake & Los Feliz
10. Hollyhock House

Hollyhock House, designed by Frank Lloyd Wright

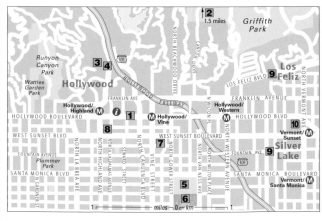

For more information on Hollywood, call up the Hollywood Visitors' Information Center at 213-689-8822

Hollywood Boulevard

1 Hollywood Boulevard
Hollywood's main artery *(see pp 10–11)*, one of the district's most glamorous streets during its pre-World War II heydays, has been revitalized in recent years. The focus of this rejuvenation is the extravagantly designed Hollywood and Highland complex, but old favorites such as Mann's Chinese Theatre and the Walk of Fame have also received a fresh sheen. ◈ *Map P2*

2 Hollywood Sign
From the very beginning, the shiny white Hollywood sign atop Mount Lee was meant to attract attention, originally for the real estate developer and publisher Harry Chandler. Built in 1923 at a cost of $21,000, the sign was once illuminated by 4,000 bulbs and had its own caretaker. Each letter is 50 ft (15 m) tall and is made of sheet metal. In 1932, unemployed actress Peggy Entwistle immortalized herself by leaping to her death off the H. It's illegal to hike to the sign, but the top of Beachwood Drive gets you fairly close to LA's most recognizable landmark. ◈ *Map D2*

3 Hollywood Bowl
A night at the world's largest natural amphitheater is as much part of Los Angeles summer tradition as backyard barbecues and fun at the beach. The world's finest artists – from Sinatra to Pavarotti – have performed here since 1922. In 1924, Lloyd Wright designed the first concert shell, greatly improving acoustics.
◈ *Map P1 • 2301 N Highland Ave • 323-850-2000 • Concerts Tue–Sun late Jun–mid-Sep (tickets required) • www.hollywoodbowl.com*

4 Hollywood Heritage Museum
This museum is housed in the 1895 barn where Jesse Lasky and Cecil B. De Mille set up Hollywood's first major film studio in 1913. Originally located at Selma Avenue and Vine Street, De Mille shot Hollywood's first full-length feature *The Squaw Man* here in 1913–14. Exhibits include a recreated studio as well as plenty of photographs, props, and memorabilia from the silent movie era. ◈ *Map P1 • 2100 N Highland Ave • 323-874-2276 • Open 11am–4pm Sat–Sun • Adm*

Hollywood Sign

 For a peek into the history of the Hollywood Bowl visit the Bowl Museum; entry is free

Hollywood Sign

Over time the Hollywood Sign lost not only its last four letters (it was originally "Hollywoodland") but also its luster along with the rest of historic Hollywood. A "save-the-sign" campaign in 1978 received the help of celebrities such as Hugh Hefner, who held a fundraiser, and Alice Cooper, who bought the second O in honor of Groucho Marx.

5 Hollywood Forever Cemetery

Founded in 1899, this cemetery has the densest concentration of celebrity corpses in the world. The long list of those interred here includes Rudolph Valentino, Jane Mansfield, and Cecil B. De Mille. The grandest memorial, though, belongs to Douglas Fairbanks Sr. who, since 2000, has shared his marble tomb with his son, Douglas Fairbanks Jr. Buy a map of the graves from the nearby flower shop. ◈ Map R3 • 6000 Santa Monica Blvd • 323-469-1181 • Open seasonal hours • Free • www. forevernetwork.com

6 Paramount Studios

The only major movie studio still located in Hollywood, Paramount traces its pedigree back to 1916 when movies were made with the Paramount logo. The studio has always had a stunning star roster and in 1929, Paramount's *Wings* took home the first ever Best Picture Oscar. More recent hits include *Psycho*, *The Godfather*, *Forrest Gump*, and *Titanic*. Studio tours have been suspended indefinitely but you can enter the ornate gates by being part of a live audience for a TV show taping. ◈ Map R4 • 5555 Melrose Ave • Closed to the public

7 Cinerama Dome

A Hollywood landmark and site of many a movie premiere, this white dome of interlocked triangles is LA's most unusual movie theater. The world's only concrete geodesic dome was built by Welton Beckett in 1963 to show Cinerama movies, a revolutionary wide-screen technique requiring three 35 mm projectors. Today, it is part of a brand new complex that also includes the ArcLight movie theaters *(see p56)*. ◈ Map Q3 • 323-464-4226 • www.arclightcinemas.com

8 Crossroads of the World

The centerpiece of this unique architectural metaphor is a shiplike Art Deco building that "sails" into a courtyard flanked by cottages in styles ranging

Hollywood Forever Cemetery

  For live taping information and reservations at Paramount Studios call 323-956-1777

Crossroads of the World

from Spanish Colonial to German gingerbread. A quiet office complex, it was built in 1936 by Robert Derrah, who designed downtown's Coca-Coca Bottling Plant *(see p77)*. ✆ *Map P3 • 6671 Sunset Blvd • Open for strolling*

9 Silver Lake & Los Feliz

The twin neighborhoods of Silver Lake and Los Feliz constitute one of Los Angeles's oldest movie colonies with bohemian-chic dining, shopping, and nightlife scenes. The hills are studded with Modernist master-pieces such as Frank Lloyd Wright's 1924 Ennis-Brown House and the Lovell House built by Richard Neutra. ✆ *Map D2 • Ennis-Brown House, 2655 Glendower Ave, 323-660-0607, Guided tours (reservations required) • Lovell House, 4616 Dundee Dr, closed to the public*

10 Hollyhock House

Los Feliz is also home to the Hollyhock House, a community arts center. The Mayan-style mansion was designed by Frank Lloyd in 1921 for oil heiress Aline Barnsdall. Depictions of the holly-hock, her favorite flower, appear everywhere on façades and in furniture. ✆ *Map D2 • 4808 Hollywood Blvd • 323-644-6269 • Open 12:30am–3:30pm Sat & Sun, weekdays: call for reservation • Adm (free for under 13s)*

A Day With the Stars

Morning

Begin at La Brea Avenue and Hollywood Boulevard, heading east to the **Hollywood Entertainment Museum** *(see p10)* for a high-tech look at movie-making, then step into the **Hollywood Roosevelt Hotel** *(see p10 & p146)*, home of the first Academy Awards. In **Mann's Chinese Theatre** *(see p56)* you can stand on the footprints of your favorite stars. An escalator will whisk you into the vast **Hollywood and Highland** complex *(see p11)* with great shopping and views of the **Hollywood Sign** and the dazzling **El Capitan** *(see p56)*. A two-block detour south on Highland Avenue takes you to **Hollywood High School**, alma mater of Lawrence Fishburne. Lana Turner was discovered at the **Top Hat Malt Shop** which once stood at the corner of Sunset and Highland. Backtrack north on Highland Avenue for a delicious retro lunch at **Mel's Drive-In** *(see p101)*.

Afternoon

Back on Hollywood Boulevard, you'll come across the exotic **Egyptian Theatre** *(see p11 & p56)* and, at No. 6667, **Musso & Frank**'s *(see p101)*, Hollywood's oldest restaurant, once the haunt of Chaplin, Hemingway, and other famous people. At **Frederick's of Hollywood** *(see p11)*, take a peek at the stars' underwear in a special exhibition. Wrap up the day with drinks and sunset views at **Yamashiro**'s *(see p100)*, followed by a grand gourmet meal at the popular **Patina** *(see p101)*.

Around Town – Hollywood

➤ Following pages **The brightly lit Mann's Chinese Theatre**

Left **A bar in Hollywood** Right **The Cat & Fiddle Pub sign**

TOP 10 Bars & Dance Clubs

1 Beauty Bar
Get your nails done while sipping a "Blue Rinse" cocktail at this unique retro bar styled like a 1950s beauty parlor. ◈ *Map Q2* • *1638 N Cahuenga Blvd* • *323-464-7676* • *www.beautybar.com*

2 Deep
This sexy club has a glass-enclosed dance floor, writhing barely-clad performers, and video-monitor-equipped VIP rooms. ◈ *Map Q2* • *1707 N Vine St* • *323-462-1144* • *Open Fri & Sat* • *www.deeptheclub.com*

3 Lava Lounge
Hidden behind heavy doors in a nondescript mini-mall, this tiki lounge features live bands. ◈ *Map P2* • *1533 N La Brea Ave* • *323-876-6612* • *www.lavahollywood.com*

4 The Highlands
This vast and trendy Hollywood and Highland club *(see p10)* boasts several dance floors and a Wolfgang Puck restaurant. ◈ *Map P2* • *6801 Hollywood Blvd* • *323-461-9800* • *Open Fri–Sat* • *www.thehighlandsla.com*

5 Cinespace
Watch a movie, munch on contemporary American cuisine, and on weekends, listen to a DJ spin house music. ◈ *Map Q2* • *6356 Hollywood Blvd* • *323-817-3456* • *www.cine-space.com*

6 Yamashiro
Gorgeous views of the city and sunset cocktails give this Japanese palace an edge. Follow with dinner in the restaurant or enjoy the small garden. ◈ *Map P2* • *1999 N Sycamore Ave* • *323-466-5125*

7 Forty Deuce
Hollywood decadence is still alive at this provocative yet classy bar where sexy dancers bare nearly all during burlesque strip shows. ◈ *Map Q4* • *5574 Melrose Ave* • *323-465-4242* • *www.fortydeuce.com*

8 Cat & Fiddle Pub
Homesick Brits mingle with midriff-baring LA scenesters. Quaff your libation on the all-Californian patio or beneath the Union Jacks and dart boards inside. Full menu. ◈ *Map Q3* • *6530 Sunset Blvd* • *323-468-3800* • *www.catandfiddle.com*

9 Formosa Café
Humphrey Bogart and Marilyn Monroe once hung out at this watering hole. Enjoy the signature *mai tais* and tasty California-Asian treats. ◈ *Map P3* • *7156 Santa Monica Blvd* • *323-850-9050*

10 Good Luck Bar
A cool crowd gathers around the oval bar or in the sofa lounge at this fashionable, Chinese-style Silver Lake watering hole. ◈ *Map D2* • *1514 Hillhurst Ave* • *323-666-3524*

Price Categories

Price categories include a three-course meal for one, a glass of house wine, and all unavoidable extra charges including tax.

$	under $25
$$	$25–$50
$$$	$50–$80
$$$$	over $80

Mel's Drive-in

🔟 Places to Eat

1 Pig'n'Whistle
This 1927 landmark reopened with its gorgeous dark wood interior beautifully restored. The menu features famous pork dishes. ◈ Map P2 • 6714 Hollywood Blvd • 323-463-0000 • Veg: Limited • $$

2 Mel's Drive-in
Those hungry for nostalgia and big juicy burgers should head to this 1950s-style diner. The original featured in the classic 1973 movie American Graffiti. ◈ Map P2 • 1650 N Highland Ave • 323-465-2111 • $

3 Ammo
Simple California comfort food is served from morning to night at this tiny but cosy minimalist café. ◈ Map P3 • 1155 N Highland Ave • 323-871-2666 • $$

4 Vert
One of Wolfgang Puck's newest outposts serves French and Italian food. You must try the bellini, a bubbly blend of green apple juice and prosecco. ◈ Map P2 • 6801 Hollywood Blvd • 323-491-1300 • Veg: Limited • $$

5 Prizzi's Piazza
Famous for its garlic breadsticks, epic wine list, big plates of pasta, and crispy thin-crust pizza. ◈ Map R2 • 5923 Franklin Ave • 323-467-0168 • $$

6 Musso & Frank Grill
Steaks and chops dominate the menu of Hollywood's oldest (since 1919) restaurant. It was a major hangout for celebrities such as Hemingway and other literary giants. ◈ Map P2 • 6667 Hollywood Blvd • 323-467-7788 • $$

7 Café Stella
This romantic, French-style eatery offers mostly outdoor seating in a lovely courtyard with hanging amber lights and olive and lavender plants. ◈ Map E2 • 3932 W Sunset Blvd • 323-666-0265 • Closed Sun & Mon • $$$

8 Pinot Hollywood
Joachim Splichal's eatery serves great Californian/French fusion cuisine. Patio and bar area with sofas. ◈ Map Q3 • 1448 N Gower St • 323-461-8800 • Closed Sun • $$$

9 Madame Matisse
Popular for breakfast, this bistro also turns out delicious French country classics for lunch and dinner. No beer or wine. ◈ Map D2 • 3536 W Sunset Blvd • 323-662-4862 • No dis. access • $

10 Yuca's Hut
Head this way for yummy Mexican food. Try the cochinita pibil tacos. ◈ Map D2 • 2056 N Hillhurst Ave, Los Feliz • 323-662-1214 • No credit cards • Veg: No • $

Unless otherwise stated, all restaurants accept credit cards, serve vegetarian meals, and provide access for the disabled

Left **Los Angeles County Museum of Art (LACMA)** Right **Petersen Automotive Museum**

West Hollywood & Midtown

WEST HOLLYWOOD IS LA'S PARTY ZONE *and teems with nightclubs, restaurants, bars, and comedy clubs. After dark, Sunset Strip is the center of the action for poseurs, producers, and the pretty. Huge, lascivious lips on Armani billboards leer down at you, and if you want to be "seen at the scene," this is the place to be. West Hollywood is also LA's "gayest" quarter, especially along Santa Monica Boulevard, where you'll find the party in full swing. For shopaholics there's Melrose Avenue, a quirky pathway lined with designer stores, tattoo parlors, Gothic-chic shops, and bustling cafés and eateries. It's also home to the Pacific Design Center, the anchor of the Avenues of Art & Design, and a treasure trove of chic home accessories. For cultural edification, head south to an amorphous district we've termed "Midtown," whose main artery, Wilshire Boulevard, boasts some of the city's finest museums along the historic Miracle Mile.*

Pacific Design Center (PDC)

🔟 Sights

1. Los Angeles County Museum of Art (LACMA)
2. Farmers Market
3. The Grove
4. Pacific Design Center (PDC)
5. Avenues of Art & Design
6. Melrose Avenue
7. Sunset Strip
8. Petersen Automotive Museum
9. Page Museum & La Brea Tar Pits
10. Crafts & Folk Art Museum (CAFAM)

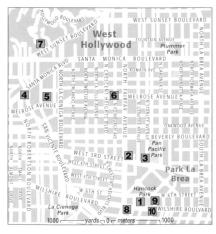

1 Los Angeles County Museum of Art (LACMA)

It's impossible not to marvel when touring the galleries of this well-respected art and culture museum. A virtual cornucopia of paintings, sculpture, furniture, and objects that would take several days to peruse awaits in six buildings. LACMA also hosts international touring exhibits *(see pp16–19)*.

The Theatres sign
at the Grove

2 Farmers Market

In 1934, two entrepreneurs asked landowner E.B. Gilmore for permission to start a produce market on a vacant parking lot on his property. Soon after, a group of farmers started selling fresh fruit, flowers, and vegetables from trucks. Many of the 150 stalls of Farmers Market, such as Magee's Nuts, have been in the same families for generations. Scouts from nearby CBS TV City roam the market in search of game show audience members. ✆ *Map M5 • 6333 W 3rd St • 323-954-4230 • Open 9am–9pm Mon–Fri, 9am–8pm Sat, 10am–7pm Sun • Free • www.farmersmarketla.com*

Farmers Market

3 The Grove

Adjoining the Farmers Market, The Grove is an attractive, upscale outdoor shopping and dining center with a first-rate 14-screen movie theater. Open since 2002, this mall features highlights such as a historic trolley connecting it with the market, a fountain that occasionally erupts into a choreographed water show set to music, and a bronze sculpture of flying angels. Along with adjacent CBS and the Farmers Market, The Grove occupies land once owned by the Gilmore family, who made their fortune from oil. Gilmore Stadium, home of the Hollywood Stars, a baseball team owned by Bing Crosby, Cecil B. De Mille, and Barbara Stanwyck, was once located where CBS now stands. ✆ *Map N5 • 189 The Grove Drive • 323-900-8000 • Open 10am–9pm Mon–Thu, 10am–10pm Fri & Sat, 11am–7pm Sun*

4 Pacific Design Center (PDC)

The 130 showrooms of this vast complex display the finest in furniture, fabrics, lighting, and accessories. A contemporary 1975 design by Cesar Pelli, the most striking feature of the PDC is the gleaming blue glass façade, which has earned it the nickname "The Blue Whale." The clover-green addition dates from 1988. On the plaza behind the PDC is a branch of the Museum of Contemporary Art *(see p72)*, showcasing architecture and design. ✆ *Map L4 • 8687 Melrose Ave, 310-657-0800, Open 9am–5pm Mon–Fri, Free • MOCA at PDC, 310-289-5223, Open 11am–5pm Tue–Fri (to 8pm Thu), 11am–6pm Sat & Sun, Adm (free Thu) • www.moca.org*

The Pacific Design Center tourist office (Suite M-38) is open 8:30am–5:30pm Mon–Fri

Gay Los Angeles
West Hollywood is the center of LA's gay and lesbian community. There's plenty of partying in the many happening bars, clubs, cafés, and restaurants along Santa Monica Boulevard. Huge crowds turn up for the colorful Christopher Street West Parade in June and the wonderfully outrageous Halloween Carnival that takes place in late October.

5 Avenues of Art & Design
The streets surrounding the PDC are flanked with design stores where you can actually buy – and not just look at (as in the PDC) – that chintz sofa or Eames chair. Best explored on foot, the district is filled with cutting-edge art galleries *(see p107)*, trendy restaurants, and cafés where you can relax over latte. ◈ *Map L4 • Along Beverly Blvd, Robertson Blvd, & Melrose Ave between La Cienega Blvd & Doheny Dr*

6 Melrose Avenue
Though it has certainly seen better days, Melrose Avenue *(see p108)* is still a haven for Hollywood hipsters and the place to stock up on vintage threads, provocative fashions, and unusual gift items. Weekend afternoons are prime time for soaking up the scene, preferably from a table at an outdoor café, delicious ice-cold frappuccino in hand.

7 Sunset Strip
Sunset Strip has been LA's nocturnal playground since the 1920s and is the most history-laden section of the 25-mile (40-km) Sunset Boulevard. Stars, starlets, wannabes, and those that like to be around them are still drawn to landmarks old and new, including the Chateau Marmont, the Whisky a Go-Go, the Mondrian Hotel with its exclusive Sky Bar, and Johnny Depp's music club, the Viper Room *(see pp8–9)*.

8 Petersen Automotive Museum
LA's evolution from sleepy outpost to sweeping megalopolis is uniquely tied to the rise of the automobile. This is the basic premise of this wonderful museum, which does a lot more than display pretty vintage cars (though there are plenty of those, too). On the ground floor, you'll follow a Los Angeles "streetscape" through 100 years of car history. You'll pass dioramas of a 1920s gas station, a 1930s showroom, and a 1950s drive-in restaurant. Upstairs, the cars take center stage. Exhibits change regularly, but usually include galleries devoted to hot rods, motorcycles, and vehicles owned by Hollywood celebrities or used in movies. For children, the Discovery Center makes science fun. ◈ *Map M6 • 6060 Wilshire Blvd, Miracle Mile • 323-930-2277 • Open 10am–6pm Tue–Sun • Adm*

Colorful shop window on Melrose Avenue

9 Page Museum & La Brea Tar Pits
You won't find mammoths, saber-toothed cats, or dire wolves in any zoo, but they are the stars of this museum offering a look at life in LA during the last

The Pit 91 Visitors Station (La Brea Tar Pits) is open 10am–4pm Wed–Sun during summer; entry is free

La Brea Tar Pits

Ice Age thousands of years ago. Since 1906, excavations at the pits adjacent to the museum have yielded more than one million fossilized bones of about 450 species, from insects to birds and mammals. Many are now on display at the museum, which also houses a glass-walled laboratory where paleontologists may be seen working. Outside the museum, life-size replicas of mammoths trapped in muck dramatize the ghastly fate of Los Angeles's prehistoric denizens. ⓢ Map N6 • 5801 Wilshire Blvd, Miracle Mile • 323-934-7243 • Open 9:30am–5pm Mon–Fri, 10am–5pm Sat & Sun • Adm • www.pagemuseum.org

10 Crafts & Folk Art Museum (CAFAM)

This small museum is dedicated to showcasing handicrafts and folk art from around the world. The brainchild of folk art collector Edith Wyle, it was originally launched in 1965 as "The Egg and The Eye," a gallery space and omelet restaurant. Apart from its changing exhibits, which reflect the multi-layered culture of Southern California, CAFAM is best known for its annual International Festival of Masks held in October. ⓢ Map N6 • 5814 Wilshire Blvd, Miracle Mile • 323-937-4230 • Open 11am–5pm Wed–Sun • Adm (free for under 12s) • www.cafam.org

A Day in Hollywood

Morning

Start your day at Wilshire Boulevard's "Museum Row" to catch the latest headline exhibit at **LACMA** (see pp16–19) or selections from its superb permanent collection. Don't miss the beautiful Pavilion for Japanese Art. If you can muster the energy before lunch, head for the **Petersen Automotive Museum** or the **Page Museum**.

Leaving Museum Row, drive a few blocks north to the **Farmers Market**. Try the Cajun food at **Gumbo Pot**, the all-American menu at the retro **Kokomo**, or the **Du-par's** diner fare.

Afternoon

For an afternoon of shopping, start with the Farmers Market itself, then wander over to **The Grove**, a new outdoor mall. Head north on Fairfax Avenue, turning right on **Melrose Avenue**. This quintessential LA shopping street is packed with fun and funky stores and offers great people-watching opportunities, especially on weekends.

Head for an early dinner at **Campanile** (see p109), where you'll be treated to innovative California cuisine, then drive to **Sunset Strip** for an evening of laughs at the **Comedy Store** (see p55) or **The Laugh Factory** (see p55). Make your reservations in advance. Showtime is usually 8pm. Round off your day with a drink at **Bar Marmont** (see p106) or the lounge at the chic **Standard Hollywood** (see p147).

Left **House of Blues** Right **The Roxy sign**

Sunset Strip Bars & Clubs

1 Bar Marmont
Super-trendy lounge next to the Chateau Marmont hotel with lots of beautiful people to gawk at. To increase your chances of getting past the front door arrive early, by about 9 or 10pm. ◈ *Map M3 • 8171 Sunset Blvd • 323-650-0575*

2 Dublin's
This cavernous Irish pub is party central thanks to strong drinks and a relatively relaxed door policy. The sports bar downstairs has pool tables and pub grub. ◈ *Map M3 • 8240 Sunset Blvd • 323-656-0100*

3 The Lounge at the Standard
The entertainment at this hotel hot spot includes performance art by a barely clothed beauty on view in a glass booth above the reception, and dancing. ◈ *Map M3 • 8300 Sunset Blvd • 323-822-3111*

4 House of Blues
The original HOB branch has an eclectic schedule of performers, including long-time favorites such as Joan Armatrading and the Bangles. The Sunday Gospel brunch is an institution. ◈ *Map M3 • 8430 Sunset Blvd • 323-848-5100*

5 Sky Bar
Famous for its poolside cocktails, celebrity crowd, and sweeping city views, getting past the velvet rope here is a tall order. ◈ *Map M3 • 8440 Sunset Blvd, at the Mondrian Hotel • 323-848-6025*

6 Saddle Ranch Chop House
A Texas-style steakhouse popular with families until 10pm, after which it becomes a lively night-time hangout complete with mechanical bull. ◈ *Map M3 • 8371 W Sunset Blvd • 323-656-2007*

7 Viper Room
Celebrity musicians such as Bruce Springsteen stage concerts at Johnny Depp's club *(see p9 & p64)*. ◈ *Map L3 • 8852 Sunset Blvd • 310-358-1880*

8 Whisky a Go-Go
LA's epicenter of rock'n'roll in the 1960s, this club was the springboard for the Doors and still books new bands. ◈ *Map L3 • 8901 W Sunset Blvd • 310-652-4202*

9 The Roxy
Serious music fans love this no-nonsense club where the focus is on the show, not the decor or the crowd. ◈ *Map K3 • 9009 W Sunset Blvd • 310-278-9457*

10 Key Club
This glitzy three-story club plays live rock as well as DJ-spun dance music. ◈ *Map K3 • 9039 W Sunset Blvd • 310-274-5800*

Left **The Margo Leavin Gallery sign** Right **George Stern Fine Arts**

TOP 10 Art Galleries

1 Margo Leavin Gallery
Margo Leavin presents contemporary American and European art and photography. Claes Oldenburg designed the sculpture "Knife Slicing Through Water" by the entrance. ◎ *Map L4* • *812 N Robertson Blvd* • *310-273-0603*

2 Chac Mool Gallery
One of LA's finest galleries for contemporary American art, its shows may feature sculpture by Los Angeles-based Robert Graham, ethereal paintings by Mary Corse, or colorful assemblages by Charles Arnoldi. ◎ *Map K4* • *8920 Melrose Ave* • *310-550-6792*

3 George Stern Fine Arts
This gallery specializes in late 19th and early 20th-century California-based Impressionist landscape painters such as Guy Rose and Maurice Brown. ◎ *Map K4* • *8920 Melrose Ave* • *310-276-2600*

4 Tasende Gallery
Modern and contemporary sculpture, drawings as well as paintings by international artists such as Eduardo Chillida or Henry Moore are on view. ◎ *Map L4* • *8808 Melrose Ave* • *310-276-8686*

5 Hamilton-Selway Gallery
Home to the largest collection of Andy Warhol originals on the West Coast, this gallery also features Roy Lichtenstein, Keith Haring, and other pop art icons. ◎ *Map L4* • *8678 Melrose Ave* • *310-657-1711*

6 Tobey C. Moss
This LA art scene fixture began with a focus on prints and drawings, but is best known as a keen promoter of pre-1960s California Modernists. ◎ *Map N5* • *7321 Beverly Blvd* • *323-933-5523*

7 Regen Projects
This unassuming space, hidden in an alley, presents cutting-edge contemporary art by emerging and established artists, such as Catherine Opie, Lari Pittman, and Richard Prince. ◎ *Map K4* • *633 N Almont Dr* • *310-276-5424*

8 Iturralde Gallery
This gallery run by the Mexican-born sisters Ana and Teresa Iturralde functions as a gateway to the US market for many modern and contemporary Latin American artists. ◎ *Map P5* • *116 S La Brea Ave* • *323-937-4267*

9 Fahey/Klein Gallery
A power in the world of rare, vintage, and contemporary art photography, Fahey/Klein showcases Henri Cartier-Bresson and other high-profile artists. ◎ *Map P5* • *148 N La Brea Ave* • *323-934-2250*

10 Jan Baum Gallery
Jan Baum is a top dealer in international and American art and represents prominent African-American artists, including the Saar family. Betye Saar designed downtown's Biddy Mason park *(see p78)*. ◎ *Map P5* • *170 S La Brea Ave* • *323-932-0170*

Left **Melrose Trading Post** Center & Right **Off the Wall Antiques sign & shop**

🔟 Shops on Melrose Avenue

1 Bodhi Tree
This esoteric bookstore specializes in New Age topics such as mysticism and astrology. Browse the shelves or attend lectures, you can even consult the resident psychic. ◈ *Map L4 • 8585 Melrose Ave • 310-659-1733*

2 Decades & Decades Too
If Rodeo Drive is out of your league, try this couture resale boutique. Downstairs you'll find lightly worn clothing, while upstairs stocks 1960s and 1970s Pucci and Courrèges. ◈ *Map M4 • 8214 Melrose Ave • 323-655-1960*

3 Fred Segal
This über-trendy house of style attracts A-list celebrities. Shop for fashionable clothes, luxurious beauty products, and gift items at steep prices *(see p64)*. ◈ *Map M4 • 8100 Melrose Ave (also at 420 Broadway, 500 Broadway) • 323-651-4129, 310-394-9814*

4 Melrose Trading Post
This cool Sunday flea market takes you back through the years with vintage fashions, collectibles, and retro furnishings. ◈ *Map M4 • At the corner of Melrose & Fairfax Aves • 323-655-7679 • Open 9am–5pm Sun • Adm (free for under 12s)*

5 Wasteland
Stylists and bargain-hunters shop for vintage clothing, accessories, and shoes at this warehouse-sized store. ◈ *Map N4 • 7428 Melrose Ave • 323-653-3028*

6 Wanna Buy a Watch?
Best known for its selection of vintage watches, this classy store now stocks contemporary watch models, antique diamond rings, and 1920s Art Nouveau baubles as well. ◈ *Map N4 • 7366 Melrose Ave • 323-653-0467*

7 LA Eyeworks
This unusual and happening store is known for featuring the most unique eyeglass designs on the planet and attracts its share of the hip crowd. ◈ *Map N4 • 7407 Melrose Ave • 323-653-8255*

8 Maya Jewelry
This small store stocks affordable jewelry, mostly silver, to adorn any body part you wish to, including toes, tongues, and belly buttons. Also has a great mask collection. ◈ *Map N4 • 7452 Melrose Ave • 323-655-2708*

9 Wound & Wound Toy Co
Wind-up toys are the specialty here, though you'll also find plenty of other budget-friendly playthings such as music boxes, tin figurines, and funny cartoon character lunch boxes. ◈ *Map N4 • 7374 Melrose Ave (also at Universal City Walk) • 323-653-6703*

10 Off the Wall Antiques
There's plenty of kitsch with classic neon signs, vintage toys, Art Deco lamps, and other collectibles at this emporium of weird Americana. ◈ *Map N4 • 7325 Melrose Ave • 323-930-1185*

Price Categories

Price categories include a three-course meal for one, a glass of house wine, and all unavoidable extra charges including tax.

$	under $25
$$	$25–$50
$$$	$50–$80
$$$$	over $80

Chaya Brasserie

🔟 Places to Eat

1 Angelini Osteria
Having cooked for the Pope and presidents, Chef Angelini now regales homesick Italians and foodies with his comfort food. ✪ *Map N5 • 7313 Beverly Blvd • 323-297-0070 • Veg: On request • $*

2 Swingers
This retro diner with its plaid booths and Andy Warhol wallpaper serves steamy chicken soup, delicious milkshakes, and bulging sandwiches until the wee hours. ✪ *Map M5 • 8020 Beverly Blvd • 323-653-5858 • $*

3 Cobras & Matadors
Compose a meal from a number of delicious tapas at this bustling *boîte*. No corkage fee if you buy the wine at the *bodega* next door. ✪ *Map N5 • 7615 W Beverly Blvd • 323-932-6178 • $$*

4 Joan's on Third
This little deli is great for gourmets on the go or out for a casual lunch. The tarragon chicken salad is excellent. ✪ *Map M5 • 8350 W 3rd St • 323-655-2285 • $*

5 Surya
Visit this Indian restaurant with decor inspired by the Hindu sun god for breads, tandoori, and curries. ✪ *Map M5 • 8048 W 3rd St • 323-653-5151 • $*

6 Alto Palato
Locals are addicted to the crispy thin-crust pizza and the tempting menu. The Wednesday

three-course *prix fixe* dinner is a steal. ✪ *Map L4 • 755 N La Cienega Blvd • 310-657-9271 • $$*

7 Chaya Brasserie
The bustling dining room and bamboo garden is a great backdrop for food that mixes French and Japanese flavors. ✪ *Map K5 • 8741 Alden Dr • 310-859-8833 • $*

8 Newsroom Café
The patio provides premier celeb-watching, and the eclectic menu brims with low-fat and vegan options. ✪ *Map L5 • 120 N Robertson Blvd • 310-652-4444 • $*

9 Campanile
The California-Mediterranean menu changes constantly, dishes such as pork loin with braised fennel are typical. ✪ *Map P6 • 624 S La Brea Ave • 323-938-1447 • $$$*

10 Rosalind's
Try the fragrant meat and vegetable stews at this Ethiopian joint. Music and dance erupt frequently. ✪ *Map P6 • 1044 S Fairfax Ave • 323-936-2486 • $*

Unless otherwise stated, all restaurants accept credit cards, serve vegetarian meals, and provide access for the disabled

109

Left **Museum of Television & Radio** Right **Beverly Hills City Hall, Civic Center**

Beverly Hills, Westwood, & Bel-Air

STAFF IN LIVERY STANDING OVER ROWS *of Rolls Royces, Tom Cruise disembarking from a stretch limo, cellphone-addicted fat-cat producers cutting poolside deals in pleasure-palace hotels, slinky young things in black – this is Beverly Hills where the smell of money drapes the very breeze. But there is more than just opulence and wealth here. Adjacent Westwood is home to UCLA, one of the finest public universities in the country. The nearby* Getty Center serenely lords above it all in its white majesty. Bel Air mansions have routinely passed from Fairbanks and Bogart to Streisand and Diaz. Beverly Hills and its environs offer glimpses into a fairytale lifestyle unattainable for most.

🔟 Sights

1. Beverly Hills Hotel
2. Rodeo Drive
3. Museum of Television & Radio
4. Beverly Hills Civic Center
5. Museum of Tolerance
6. University of California, Los Angeles (UCLA)
7. UCLA Hammer Museum
8. Pierce Bros Westwood Village Memorial Park
9. Skirball Cultural Center
10. Getty Center

Rodeo Drive

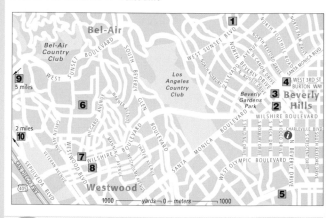

Beverly Hills Hotel

1 Beverly Hills Hotel

LA's most famous hotel *(see p146)* has been part of Hollywood history since its 1912 opening. Douglas Fairbanks Sr. and Will Rogers got drunk in the bar, Howard Hughes rented Bungalow 3 for 30 years, and Marilyn Monroe reportedly romanced both JFK and RFK here. Political leaders, royals, and Hollywood headliners have all stayed, partied, and cavorted at the legendary Pink Palace. It's been featured in movies and on the cover of the Eagles' *Hotel California* album. And stars still come – Elton John celebrated his 55th birthday here in 2002. ◈ *Map J4 • 9641 Sunset Blvd • 310-276-2251 • www.beverlyhillshotel.com*

2 Rodeo Drive

Rodeo Drive *(see p52 & p114)* is one of the world's most famous – and expensive – shopping streets, synonymous with a lifestyle of luxury and fame. Only three blocks long, it is essentially an haute couture runway, with all the major international players represented.

You'll often spot nicely groomed shoppers, though actual star sightings are rare. Rodeo's southern end is punctuated by the Regent Beverly Wilshire, one of LA's grandest hotels *(see p144)*. Architecture fans check out Frank Lloyd Wright's Anderton Court *(see p114)*. ◈ *Rodeo Drive between Wilshire & Santa Monica Blvds*

3 Museum of Television & Radio

Most people alive today have grown up watching television, one of the defining media of the 20th century. This museum, housed in a striking building by Getty Center architect Richard Meier, has made it its mission to collect, preserve, and share nearly 80 years of radio and TV history. About 120,000 programs – news to musicals, sports to sitcoms – have been catalogued and are available for viewing and listening. The museum also offers daily presentations in its on-site theaters and organizes seminars and live radio broadcasts. ◈ *Map J5 • 465 N Beverly Dr • 310-786-1000 • Open noon–5pm Wed–Sun • Donation • www.mtr.org*

4 Beverly Hills Civic Center

The wealth of a city is often reflected in its public buildings, so it should come as no surprise that Beverly Hills has the kind of civic center that's the envy of other towns. Its centerpiece is the elegant City Hall, built in 1932 in Spanish Renaissance style and harmoniously incorporated into a contemporary Spanish-style complex with palm-lined walkways and curved colonnades. It houses a beautiful library as well as the local police and fire departments. ◈ *Map J5 • East of Crescent Dr between Santa Monica Blvd & Burton Dr*

Beverly Hills by Numbers

Wealthy Beverly Hills still surprises in some aspects. Its well-heeled denizens are – two to one – registered Democrats. They really love their kids and spend 28% more every year than the state's average to educate them. And with an unemployment rate near 3%, these natives continue raking in their average $65,507 per capita incomes.

5 Museum of Tolerance

This high-tech museum confronts visitors with issues of extreme intolerance to make them realize the need for greater acceptance in today's world. The experience begins at the "Tolerancenter," whose exhibits address issues such as human rights violations and the Civil Rights movement. The Holocaust section, at the core, chronicles Nazi atrocities. A new multimedia exhibit follows the lives of well-known Americans from different ethnic backgrounds. ⊗ *Map D2 • 9786 W Pico Blvd • 310-553-8403 • Open 11:30am–4pm Mon–Thu, until 1pm Fri (until 3pm Apr–Oct), until 5pm Sun • Adm • www.museumoftolerance.com*

6 University of California, Los Angeles (UCLA)

One of the nation's top research universities, UCLA (founded in 1919) counts many luminaries among its alumni, including Francis Ford Coppola. It has around 150 buildings with architectural gems such as Royce Hall. The Fowler Museum has a marvellous collection of non-Western art. To the north is the lovely Franklin D. Murphy Sculpture Garden (see p43). ⊗ *Map C2 • Bounded by Sunset Blvd & Le Conte, Hilgard, & Gayley Aves • 310-825-4321 • www.ucla.edu*

7 UCLA Hammer Museum

This museum, run by UCLA, is the legacy of Armand Hammer, an oil tycoon who discovered a passion for collecting art in the 1920s. Hammer was especially fond of 19th-century French Impressionists such as Monet. Rotating exhibitions are complemented by traveling shows with a more contemporary angle. Free readings, film screenings, and lectures are quite popular. An upcoming renovation may require temporary full or partial closure of the museum. ⊗ *Map C2 • 10899 Wilshire Blvd • 310-443-7000 • Open 11am–7pm Tue–Sat, until 9pm Thu, 11am–5pm Sun • Adm (free for under 17s, free students with ID, free Thu) • www.hammer.ucla.edu*

8 Pierce Brothers Westwood Village Memorial Park

This small cemetery beneath Westwood's towering office high-rises has more Hollywood stars per square yard than any other burial ground in LA. Marilyn Monroe's remains rest in an above-ground crypt always decorated with flowers (Hugh Hefner has allegedly reserved the adjacent space). Other celebs buried here are Burt Lancaster, Natalie Wood, and Frank Zappa. ⊗ *Map C2 • 1218 Glendon Ave • 310-474-1579 • Open 8am–sunset*

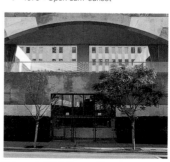

Entrance to UCLA, Hammer Museum

 The Fowler Museum at UCLA is open noon–5pm Wed–Sun (until 8pm Thu); entry is free

Skirball Cultural Center

9 Skirball Cultural Center
This state-of-the-art Jewish cultural center was named after its main benefactor, Jack Skirball (1896–1985), a rabbi and producer of Hitchcock films. Open since 1996, the complex hosts a lively events schedule and has a multimedia museum. Exhibits explore the parallels between the Jewish experience and the principles of American democracy. After a major expansion, expected to be completed in 2004, the Skirball will host a major exhibition on Albert Einstein. Ⓢ Map C2 • 2701 N Sepulveda Blvd, Brentwood/Bel-Air • 310-440-4500 • Open noon–5pm Tue–Sat, 11am–5pm Sun • Adm (free for under 12s)

10 Getty Center
Although best known for its collection of European art, the Getty offers much more – a hilltop setting with sweeping views from the ocean to the mountains, architecture as exquisite as "frozen music" (to quote Goethe), and landscaped gardens that are nothing less than the finest art (see pp12–15).

Tour of Stars' Homes

Morning

🕐 Begin your tour of stars' homes by driving north on Walden Drive, just off Santa Monica Boulevard, for a glimpse of "**Witch's House**" at the corner of Carmelita Avenue, famous for its Hansel-and-Gretel looks. Go right on Lomitas Avenue, then left on Linden Drive where mobster Bugsy Siegel was gunned down at **No. 810** in 1947. Follow Linden north to Sunset Boulevard, turn right, then left on Roxbury Avenue for two star-packed blocks. Apart from Jimmy Stewart who lived at **No. 918**, you'll also see the former homes of song lyricist Ira Gershwin (**No. 1021**), Diane Keaton (**No. 1025**), singer Rosemary Clooney (aunt of George, at **No. 1019**), Peter Falk (**No. 1004**), comedian Jack Benny (**No. 1002**), and Lucille Ball (**No. 1000**).

Turn right on Cañon Drive, then right again on Bedford Drive where the house at **No. 904** was at different times the homes of stars such as Frank Sinatra, Rex Harrison, Anthony Quinn, Greta Garbo, and Ava Gardner. Steve Martin used to live at **No. 721** and Lana Turner at **No. 730**. It was here in 1958 that Lana's daughter Cheryl Crane is believed to have killed her mother's mobster-lover Johnny Stompanato. At **No. 512** is the former home of silent screen siren Clara Bow where, in 1927, she allegedly "entertained" the entire USC football team, including Marion Morrison, better known by his screen name of John Wayne.

Left **Two Rodeo** Center **The Tiffany & Co sign** Right **Lalique lamp**

Temptations on Rodeo Drive

1 Two Rodeo
This cobbled lane resembles an idealized European shopping avenue with fountains, street lamps, and a piazza. When it opened in 1990, it was the first new street in Beverly Hills since 1914. ⓢ *Map J6 • Rodeo Dr at Wilshire Blvd*

A Gucci cushion

2 Tiffany & Co
The meticulously crafted jewelry is as exquisite as Audrey Hepburn was in the movie *Breakfast at Tiffany's*, based on the famous store in New York. ⓢ *Map J5 • 210 N Rodeo Dr • 310-273-8880*

3 Lalique
Best known for its exquisite crystal pieces, this boutique actually stocks the entire product line, including jewelry, watches, and perfume. ⓢ *Map J5 • 317 N Rodeo Dr • 310-271-7892*

4 David Orgell
A Rodeo Drive fixture since 1958, this luxury emporium is famous for its antique silver, unique jewelry, and limited edition designer watches. ⓢ *Map J5 • 320 N Rodeo Dr • 310-273-6660*

5 Anderton Court
One of Frank Lloyd Wright's later buildings (1953), the zig-zagging ramp cradling a well of light is reminiscent of the New York Guggenheim Museum. ⓢ *Map J5 • 333 N Rodeo Dr*

6 Gucci
The store is a sure-fire winner in the looks department, but most customers have eyes only for the trademark shoes, handbags, and accessories. ⓢ *Map J5 • 347 N Rodeo Dr • 310-278-3451*

7 Harry Winston
On Oscar night, when the stars come out dripping with diamonds, they're most likely on loan from the family-owned Harry Winston, one of the world's most exclusive jewelers. ⓢ *Map J5 • 371 N Rodeo Dr • 310-271-8554*

8 Bijan
This boutique stocks quality menswear, said to be the world's most expensive. Client names from Prince Charles to Steven Spielberg are etched into the window. ⓢ *Map J5 • 420 N Rodeo Dr • 310-273-6544 • Open by appointment*

9 The Rodeo Collection
A white marble outdoor shopping mall with five floors of fashion, interior design, and jewelry boutiques orbiting a sunken atrium courtyard with a fancy eatery. ⓢ *Map J5 • 421 N Rodeo Dr*

10 O'Neill House
Completed in 1988, this complex sports whimsical Art Nouveau design elements borrowed from Catalan architect Antonio Gaudí. ⓢ *Map J5 • 507 N Rodeo Dr • Not open to the public*

Price Categories

Price categories include a three-course meal for one, a glass of house wine, and all unavoidable extra charges including tax.

$	under $25
$$	$25–$50
$$$	$50–$80
$$$$	over $80

Crustacean

🔟 Places to Eat

1 Spago Beverly Hills
Stargazers are likely to report sightings when dining at Wolfgang Puck's flagship restaurant, one of the pioneers of California cuisine. ◎ *Map K5 • 176 N Cañon Dr • 310-385-0880 • $$$*

2 Crustacean
A Beverly Hills hot spot, this French Colonial restaurant serves refined Vietnamese cuisine. Try anything made with owner/chef's "secret spices." ◎ *Map J5 • 9646 S Santa Monica Blvd • 310-205-8990 • $$$*

3 Kate Mantalini
This busy upscale diner in the heart of Beverly Hills serves standard American fare including chicken pot pie, meatloaf and power breakfasts. ◎ *Map K6 • 9101 Wilshire Blvd • 310-278-3699 • $$*

4 Polo Lounge
The menu of this Beverly Hills Hotel restaurant mixes signature dishes such as McCarthy salad with healthy Asian and hearty California cuisine. ◎ *Map J4 • 9641 Sunset Blvd • 310-276-2251 • Veg: On request • $$*

5 Versailles
Lemon and garlic roasted chicken is the star at this unassuming Cuban restaurant. A must have. ◎ *Map D2 • 1415 S La Cienega Blvd (also at 10319 Venice Blvd, Culver City) • 310-289-0392 • Veg: Limited • $$*

6 Natalee Thai
Peruse the entertaining menu, then choose from various Thai classics that are served family-style. ◎ *Map L6 • 998 S Robertson Blvd (also at 10101 Venice Blvd, Culver City) • 310-855-9380 • $*

7 Matsuhisa
This is the original of Nobu Matsuhisa's small but growing empire of Japanese-Peruvian seafood restaurants. Ignore the menu and surrender to the chef's imagination. ◎ *Map L5 • 129 N La Cienega Blvd • 310-659-9639 • $$$*

8 Nate'n'Al
This modest kosher deli has been catering to the stars since 1943. Regulars swear by the huge sandwiches served on chunky rye bread. ◎ *Map J5 • 414 N Beverly Dr • 310-274-0101 • $*

9 Xi'an
For a light and tasty take on classic Chinese dishes, head to this stylish place with an outdoor patio. Try the marvelous black bean sauce and the Peking duck.
◎ *Map J5 • 362 N Cañon Dr • 310-275-3345 • $$*

10 Il Cielo
Book a romantic table beneath a star-lit sky in the enchanting garden and enjoy the classic and delicious fare. ◎ *Map K5 • 9018 Burton Way • 310-276-9990 • Closed Sun • $$*

Unless otherwise stated, all restaurants accept credit cards, serve vegetarian meals, and provide access for the disabled

115

Left **Entrance to Santa Monica Pier** Center **Venice Boardwalk** Right **Venice Canal**

Santa Monica Bay

SANTA MONICA BAY SPANS ABOUT *20 miles (32 km) between two of the richest communities in California – Malibu and Palos Verdes. It's truly the "Gold Coast" of the Golden State, and its shores have some of the finest beaches anywhere, including Topanga, Santa Monica, and Venice on through Manhattan, Hermosa, Redondo, and Torrance. American surfing, and the youth culture it spawned, was born here. In the movies, these fabled beaches have stood in for everything from Guadalcanal and Tahiti to Shangri-la. The rows of mammoth palms along the Santa Monica promenade cliffs epitomize California. Access to the Pacific along the beaches – whether by ferry to Catalina Island, surfing, taking a gondola cruise through the canals of Long Beach, or just popping into the local waves from a newly discovered favorite strand – is bountiful. Take the plunge! Santa Monica's main attraction however, is Santa Monica Pier which offers sundry entertainment options and a lively carnival atmosphere.*

🔟 Sights

Malibu Adamson House

1 Malibu Adamson House & Malibu Lagoon Museum

Located on a bluff overlooking the Malibu Lagoon, this Spanish Colonial-style mansion was built by Rhoda Rindge Adamson and her husband, Merritt, in 1928. The complex showcases hand-painted ceramic tiles manufactured by Malibu Potteries, owned by the Rindge family. The Rindges also built the Malibu Colony, a celebrity enclave now home to Tom Hanks and Barbra Streisand. The Malibu Lagoon Museum next to the Adamson House chronicles Malibu's history, from its Chumash Indian origins to its position as movie star Shangri-la. ✪ Map A3 • 23200 Pacific Coast Hwy, Malibu, 310-456-8432 • Adamson House, Open 11am–3pm Wed–Sat (last tour 2pm), Adm • Malibu Lagoon Museum, Open 11am– 3pm, Adm (free for under 18s)

Intricate tile detail in Adamson House

2 Santa Monica Pier

For a variety of entertainment, visit Santa Monica Pier. Where else can you hop on to a historic carousel, visit an aquarium, or ride a roller coaster? California's oldest amusement pier (built in 1908) also marks the western terminus of Route 66. Its oldest attraction is the 1916 Hippodrome, a merry-go-round that has made many movie appearances. Its newest is Pacific Park, a compact amusement park, anchored by a solar-powered Ferris wheel. Tucked beneath the pier, the Santa Monica Pier Aquarium is a small, family-oriented facility where you can observe and pet local marine life. ✪ Map A4 • At the end of Colorado Ave • Hippodrome, 310-395-4248 • Pacific Park, 310-260-8744 • Ocean Discovery Center, 310-393-6149

3 Bergamot Station Arts Center

This former historic trolley station has been imaginatively recycled into an industrial-flavored complex of nearly three dozen galleries, shops, artists' studios, and a café. A highlight is the Santa Monica Art Museum, exhibiting cutting-edge artists, many of whom work in non-traditional media including video installations. It also organizes lectures, workshops, and other events designed to involve the community in the creative process. ✪ Map B4 • 2525 Michigan Ave, Santa Monica, 310-586-6488, Open 11am–6pm Tue–Sat, Donation, www.smmoa.org • Galleries, Open 10am–6pm Tue–Sat, Free

4 Third Street Promenade

Downtown Santa Monica's main artery, this three-block mall is one of the most pleasant walking areas in LA. The product of a hugely successful

Poster on display in Bergamot Station

Around Town – Santa Monica Bay

 Third Street Promenade and Main Street in Santa Monica are great for walking

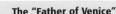

The "Father of Venice"

Venice sprang from the vision of tobacco magnate Abbot Kinney (1850–1920), who transformed the soggy marshland lying south of Santa Monica into a canal-laced, oceanfront theme park complete with gondolas and an amusement pier. It opened on July 4, 1905, and was a grand success until fire destroyed most of the theme park facilities in 1920.

revitalization effort in the late 1980s, it is flanked by upscale shops, movie theaters, and eclectic restaurants, bars, and cafés. Street musicians from around the globe shower strollers with flamenco, jazz, and hip hop. On Wednesday and Saturday mornings, the farmers market attracts large crowds.
⊗ Map A4 • 3rd St between Broadway & Wilshire Blvd, Santa Monica

5 Venice Boardwalk

It is perhaps fitting that Venice Beach, masterminded by an eccentric visionary named Abbot Kinney (see box), is LA's epicenter of counterculture. The circus-like scene reigning along the seaside boardwalk (officially known as "Ocean Front Walk") must be seen to be believed (see p122). Avoid after dark.
⊗ Map A5 • Ocean Front Walk between Venice Blvd & Rose Ave

6 Venice Canals

Abbot Kinney's Venice of America was once laced with 16 miles (26 km) of canals. The area languished until the 1960s when beatniks such as Stuart Perkoff discovered its unique charm, dragging flower children – most famously Jim Morrison – in their wake. In 1994, the city restored 3 miles (5 km) of canals, which have since become a beautiful,

upscale neighborhood. A narrow walkway that is known as the Venice Canal Walk threads through here. ⊗ Map A6 • Between Washington & Venice Blvds

7 Marina del Rey

With over 6,000 yachts and pleasure boats, Marina del Rey is the largest small-craft harbor in the world and the place to come for those seeking fun on the water. Active types could explore the harbor on kayaks. You can also catch a dinner cruise, book a whale-watching trip (January to March), or charter a sport fishing boat. Favorite landlubber activities include a sunset dinner at one of the many excellent restaurants. ⊗ Map C3 • South of Venice Beach • Visitors Bureau • 4701 Admiralty Way • 310-305-9545

8 South Bay

Surfing, swimming, tanning, beach volleyball, and other outdoor pursuits govern the laid-back lifestyle of the string of three picture-perfect beach towns in the southern Santa Monica Bay. Of these, Manhattan Beach (see p45) is the most sophisti-

Yachts in the harbor at Marina del Rey

Hermosa Beach, South Bay

cated, Hermosa (see p45) the liveliest, and Redondo the most historical. A paved trail paralleling the beach and connecting all the three communities is perfect for bicycling and inline skating. ◈ Map C5

9 Palos Verdes Peninsula

This posh enclave straddling a rocky precipice is one of the most exclusive in America. A drive along its coastline affords great ocean views with Catalina Island (see pp36–7) in the distance. Malaga Cove and Abalone Cove are popular for tidepool explorations and Point Vicente for whale-watching. Flower lovers should head inland to the sprawling South Coast Botanic Garden. ◈ Map D6 • Follow Palos Verdes Dr along the coast • Point Vicente Lighthouse, 31501 Palos Verdes Dr West • South Coast Botanic Garden, 26300 Crenshaw Blvd

10 Wayfarer's Chapel

The most famous structure by Lloyd Wright is a striking 1951 glass and stone memorial to 18th-century theologian Emanuel Swedenborg. The chapel, overlooking the Pacific, is surrounded by landscaped grounds that include a reflecting pool and terraced amphitheater (see p40). ◈ Map D6 • 5755 Palos Verdes Dr South • 310-377-7919 • Open 8am–5pm • Free

A Day at the Beach

Morning

Start your day with a drive north along the Pacific Coast Highway for glorious ocean views. Travel to sheltered **Paradise Cove** for breakfast at the beachfront restaurant, followed by a couple of hours of frolicking in the surf or a few miles north at **Zuma Beach** (see p44). Head back south, stopping at **Malibu Adamson House** to admire beautiful ceramic tiles before walking over to **Surfrider Beach** (see p44) to watch the world's finest surfers in action.

Then it's off to **Santa Monica**. Stroll beneath the towering palms of the bluff-top **Palisades Park** (see p43) with the ocean at your feet. For better views of city and sea, treat yourself to a ride on the Ferris wheel on **Santa Monica Pier** and perhaps a snack from one of the many vendors.

Afternoon

For the rest of the afternoon, rent a bicycle and become part of LA's beach scene during an easy ride south to Venice along the paved beachfront bike trail. Park the bike or push it along the bizarre **Venice Boardwalk** (see p122), perhaps stopping to get a tattoo (henna or ink), visit a fortune teller, stock up on unique souvenirs, or tank up on gourmet sausages from **Jodi Maroni's** (see p122). If time permits, continue south to **Marina del Rey**, one of the world's largest yacht harbors, before heading back to Santa Monica where myriad dinner options await.

Around Town – Santa Monica Bay

 Following pages **View of Point Vicente Lighthouse in the Palos Verdes Peninsula**

Left **Venice Pier** Center **Muscle Beach Venice** Right **Sidewalk Café**

🔟 Venice Boardwalk Attractions

1 Venice Pier
Abbott Kinney built Venice's first pier back in 1905, but the current model dates from 1963. Rescued from demolition in the mid-1980s, the restored fishing pier reopened in 1997.

2 Murals
Numerous murals beautify façades all along the Venice Boardwalk and its side streets. Rip Cronk's *Venice Reconstituted* and *Homage to a Starry Night* are famous. ❂ Venice Reconstituted, *25 Windward Ave at Speedway* • Starry Night, *Boardwalk at Wavecrest Ave*

3 Muscle Beach Venice
Check out beefy, hunky bodybuilders with abs of steel at this outdoor gym, successor to the Santa Monica original, which shut in 1959.

4 Basketball Courts
The game's always on at Venice's famous outdoor courts, especially during "Hoops by the Beach," which draws the best street basketball teams.

5 Street Performers
The best in the business, Boardwalk's street performers dance, walk barefoot on glass, balance people on their chin, and even juggle chainsaws.

6 Drum Circle
People of all colors and ages gather on the beach on Sunday afternoons, chanting and gyrating to the seductive rhythms of pots, bells, and bottles.

7 Windward Avenue
Flanking Windward Avenue are Venice's oldest Renaissance-style buildings, including St. Marks Hotel, a hostel.

8 Beach Architecture
Unique private homes line the Boardwalk between Venice and Washington Boulevards. Look for the one by Steven Ehrlich at No. 2311 and Frank Gehry's Norton House.

9 Jody Maroni's Sausage Kingdom
The simple sausage goes gourmet at this locally popular but unassuming take-out stand. ❂ 2011 Ocean Front Walk • 310-822-5639

10 Sidewalk Café
The kitchen produces satisfying sandwiches, salads, and other simple fare. Ideal for people-watching. ❂ 1401 Ocean Front Walk • 310-399-5547

Homage to a Starry Night mural

The annual "Hoops by the Beach" basketball tournament is held in May every year

Left **Shops lining Main Street** Right **MOCA Store**

Top 10 Unique Main Street Boutiques

1 Angel City Books
Bookworms in search of rare and out-of-print books may find what they're looking for. A great café next door. ✆ *Map A5 • 218 Pier Ave, just off Main St • 310-399-8767*

2 Patagonia
This is the first retail outlet of the maker of innovative outdoor clothing fit for any environment, deserts to the Everest. ✆ *Map A5 • 2936 Main St • 310-314-1776*

3 Splash
Have fun in the bathroom with handmade body products scented to suit your mood, such as the banana shake body lotion. ✆ *Map A5 • 2823 Main St • 310-581-4200*

4 Paris 1900
This boudoir-like boutique specializes in lovely romantic antique garments and matching jewelry, accessories, and lacy linens. Even the architecture of the building recalls the joyous frivolity of the Art Nouveau period. ✆ *Map A5 • 2703 Main St • 310-396-0405 • Open by appointment*

5 Arts & Letters
This lovely stationery store stocks hundreds of artist-made greeting cards, pens, and guest books. They also create custom-made invitations. ✆ *Map A5 • 2665 Main St • 310-392-9076*

6 Eames Office Gallery
This gallery and gift shop is dedicated to the first couple of Modernist design, Charles and Ray Eames. Look specially for Eames-related items. ✆ *Map A5 • 2665 Main St • 310-396-5991*

7 ZJ Boarding House
This store is for people with a passion for boards – the surf, skate, or snow variety. The knowledgeable staff help to pick through the huge selection of gear and fashion. ✆ *Map A5 • 2619 Main St • 800-205-7795*

8 Precious Metal Arts
Aspiring jewelers can learn the tricks of the trade during workshops and classes. Glass cases are filled with unique pieces that are for sale. ✆ *Map A5 • 2510 Main St • 310-581-4844*

9 MOCA Store
A smaller branch of the gift shop at MOCA in downtown LA *(see p72)*, this is a great place for artsy souvenirs, from posters to jewelry. ✆ *Map A5 • 2447 Main St • 310-396-9833*

10 Prototypes Thrift Store
This treasure trove for bargain hunters stocks quality used women's clothing, shoes, bags, and household items. Proceeds benefit a charity. ✆ *Map A4 • 2400 Main St • 310-314-1943*

Left **Inline Skating** Center **Beach Bike Trail** Right **Surfing**

Outdoor Pursuits

1 Hiking
Around 600 miles (1,000 km) of hiking trails meander through the Santa Monica Mountains, stretching from Griffith Park in Hollywood to the north of Malibu. Will Rogers State Park and Topanga State Park are good gateways for hiking.

2 Inline Skating
Enjoy skating along this 22-mile (35-km) paved trail parallel to the beach from Temescal Canyon Road north of Santa Monica to Torrance Beach. Rental outfitters are abundant in both Santa Monica and Venice.

3 Bicycling
The paved beach path (see above) is equally popular for slow bike cruises. Mountain bikers have plenty of trails to explore in the Santa Monica Mountains.

4 Hang-Gliding
Learn to take to the skies while training on beachside "bunny" hills or launch from a height of 3,500 ft (1,000 m) on a breathtaking flight with an instructor. ◎ Windsports • 818-367-2430 • www.windsports.com

5 Sailing
Skipper around the marina or cruise out to the open ocean with your very own sailboat. Rental outfits usually have a variety for you to choose from. ◎ Marina Boat Rentals: Fisherman's Village, Marina del Rey, 310-574-2822

6 Kayaking
One of the nicest places for sea kayaking is off the coast of Catalina Island (see pp36–7). Traveling leisurely by yourself allows you to explore its craggy coastline and to discover your own secret cove.

7 Surfing
The archetypal California watersport is practiced all along the coast – Surfrider Beach (see p44) in Malibu is one of the most famous, but Manhattan Beach (see p45) and Palos Verdes (see p119) are equally popular.

8 Boogie Boarding
Enjoy the thrill of the waves while riding a boogie board to the shore. It's easy and fun. All the towns on the beach have rental stations on or near the sand.

9 Windsurfing
Cabrillo Beach (see p45), nicknamed "Hurricane Gulch," is LA's windsurfing mecca. The harbor side is good for beginners, while advanced surfers can make for the open ocean. ◎ Captain Kirk's (for gear rental & lessons) • 310-833-3397

10 Fishing
Fishing without a license is permitted off any ocean pier. Sport fishing boats leave from Fisherman's Village in Marina del Rey (see p118), Shoreline Village in Long Beach, and Ports O' Call Village (see p127) in San Pedro.

Price Categories

Price categories include a
three-course meal for one,
a glass of house wine,
and all unavoidable extra
charges including tax.

$	under $25
$$	$25–$50
$$$	$50–$80
$$$$	over $80

Wall murals in Border Grill

🔟 Places to Eat

1 Inn of the Seventh Ray
Tucked away in leafy Topanga Canyon, this creekside retreat offers organic vegetarian, fish, and chicken dishes seasoned with a generous sprinkling of New Age philosophy. ◈ Map B3 • 128 Old Topanga Canyon Rd, off Pacific Coast Hwy • 310-455-1311 • $$$

2 Father's Office
This old neighborhood bar has good microbrews and tapas, although regulars swear by the gourmet burger. Delicious fries. ◈ Map C3 • 1018 Montana Ave, Santa Monica • 310-393-2337 • $

3 Border Grill
Chefs Mary Sue Milliken and Susan Feniger serve up their unique blend of Mexican flavors. Try the delicious rock shrimp *ceviche*. ◈ Map A4 • 1445 4th St, Santa Monica • 310-451-1655 • $$

4 17th Street Café
Located in the ritziest part of Santa Monica, this low-key favorite borrows from Italian, French, and Mexican cuisines. ◈ Map C3 • 1610 Montana Ave, Santa Monica • 310-453-2771 • $

5 Mao's Kitchen
Chinese food served to an eclectic crowd in a funky-stylish dining room. No alcohol. ◈ Map A6 • 1512 Pacific Ave, Venice • 310-581-8305 • $

6 Joe's
Joe's has the feel of a neighborhood eatery but fills up nightly with discerning diners from all over town who love Joe Miller's exciting California-French concoctions. ◈ Map A5 • 1023 Abbott Kinney Blvd, Venice • 310-399-5811 • $$$

7 26 Beach Restaurant
This neighborhood restaurant serves generous portions of American and Continental cuisine in a romantic setting. Specialties include large burgers, pastas and salads. ◈ Map A5 • 3100 Washington Blvd, Venice • 310-823-7526 • $

8 The Kettle
This upscale coffee shop serves delicious home-style cooking, including omelets and hearty French onion soup. Family-friendly and open 24 hours. ◈ Map C4 • 1138 Highland Ave, Manhattan Beach • 310-545-8511 • $

9 Uncle Bill's Pancake House
The pancakes and omelets are good, and the tasty French toast, burgers, and salads very popular. ◈ Map C4 • 1305 Highland Ave, Manhattan Beach • 310-545-5177 • $

10 Chez Melange
The menu offers a United Nations of dishes, from sushi to kebab and schnitzel. ◈ Map D5 • 1716 S Pacific Coast Highway, Redondo Beach • 310-540-1222 • $

Unless otherwise stated, all restaurants accept credit cards, serve vegetarian meals, and provide access for the disabled

Left **Shoreline Village** Right **Museum of Latin American Art (MOLAA)**

Long Beach & San Pedro

SAN PEDRO AND LONG BEACH *are the maritime muscles fueling LA's reputation as a great trading city. San Pedro supplies much of the manpower that operates the cranes, derricks, tugs, and railway systems in one of the most awesome seaports in the world. Through here pass the goods – automobiles, electronics, and foods – that will make their way to virtually every city in the Americas and Asia. Long Beach, on the other hand, is a city in metamorphosis. Shedding its working-class past, it has become a sophisticated cultural and financial hub. Long Beach's pulse beats strongest along Pine Avenue where indulgences range from Italian Barolo wines to music by Berlioz and belly dance. The grand ocean liner* Queen Mary *and a defining aquarium are the area's flagship sights.*

🔟 Sights

1. Cabrillo Marine Aquarium
2. Los Angeles Maritime Museum
3. Ports O' Call Village
4. Banning Residence Museum
5. Queen Mary
6. Aquarium of the Pacific
7. Museum of Latin American Art (MOLAA)
8. Long Beach Museum of Art
9. Naples & Belmont Shore
10. Ranchos Los Alamitos & Los Cerritos

Canal in residential Naples

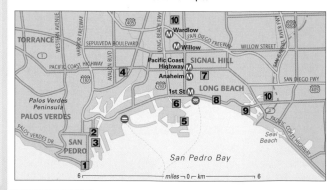

Cabrillo Marine Aquarium

Cabrillo Marine Aquarium

Housed in a modern building designed by Frank Gehry, this aquarium *(see p51)* offers plenty to do apart from viewing marine life in its 34 saltwater tanks. Memorable experiences include observing newborn jellyfish in the aquatic nursery, listening to whale sounds, and viewing prickly urchins and sea stars in tidepools accessed through the short Cabrillo Coastal Park Trail. 🅢 *Map D6 • 3720 Stephen White Drive, San Pedro • 310-548-7562 • Open noon–5pm Tue–Fri, 10am–5pm Sat–Sun • Donation • www.cabrilloaq.org*

Los Angeles Maritime Museum

This Art Deco museum celebrates LA's seafaring tradition through displays of ship models, photographs, nautical equipment, and memorabilia. A highlight is the exhibit about the USS *Los Angeles*, a navy cruiser that saw battle in China and during the Korean War. A recreated 18-ft (5.4-m) model of the ill-fated *Titanic* is a crowd pleaser. 🅢 *Map E6 • Berth 84, at foot of 6th St, San Pedro • 310-548-7618 • Open 10am–4:30pm Tue–Sat, noon–4:30pm Sun • Donation • www.lamaritimemuseum.org*

Figurehead of Queen Victoria in Los Angeles Maritime Museum

Ports O' Call Village

This is a mock New England seaside village geared to catering to tourists. A cobblestone walkway links a variety of shops selling crafts and kitsch. There are also several restaurants, many of them with harbor views. Dine on platters of fresh shrimp, fried calamari rings, and whatever has been freshly caught that morning. For close-up views of supertankers and cargo and cruise ships, join a harbor cruise, which departs from the village. Whale-watching cruises operate from January to March. 🅢 *Map E6 • San Pedro waterfront, Berth 77 • 310-732-7696*

Banning Residence Museum

The Greek Revival style home of Phineas Banning (1830–85), the "Father of Los Angeles Harbor," offers a glimpse into the life of one of the most influential of the city's pioneers. Tours take in the office, parlor, family and dining rooms, kitchen, and nursery, all filled with late 19th-century period furniture. 🅢 *Map E5 • 401 E M St, Wilmington 310-548-7777 • Donation • www.banningmuseum.org*

Tours at the Banning Residence Museum start at 12:30pm, 1:30pm, & 2:30pm Tue–Thu & Sat–Sun, & 3:30pm Sat–Sun

LA's Ports

The twin harbors of Los Angeles and Long Beach are the nation's busiest, and if combined, would be surpassed only by the harbors of Hong Kong and Singapore. In an average year, over 10 million containers worth about $200 billion come through here. Over 90 percent of all trade is with Asia, especially China, Japan, and South Korea.

Queen Mary

5 On its maiden voyage in 1936, the *Queen Mary* was the most luxurious liner ever to sail the seven seas. Each crossing carried famous faces, along with thousands of regular vacationers and immigrants. During World War II, she whisked as many as 15,000 soldiers per trip from the USA to Europe. The elegant vessel retired in 1964 and became a tourist attraction three years later. Much of the *Queen Mary*, which also contains a hotel, can be explored on self-guided and guided tours *(see p130)*. ◈ *Map E6 • 1126 Queen Highway, Long Beach • 562-435-3511 • Open 10am–6pm • Adm • www.queenmary.com*

Queen Mary

Aquarium of the Pacific

6 One of Long Beach's flagship attractions, this high-tech zoo teems with 12,000 fish, birds, and mammals that make their home in the Pacific Ocean. A full-scale model of a blue whale greets visitors in the Great Hall. You'll come face to face with exotic giant spider crabs, playful sea otters, and even get to pet a shark. For a look at what it takes to keep the aquarium afloat, take a Behind-the-Scenes-Tour. ◈ *Map E6 • 100 Aquarium Way, Long Beach • 562-590-3100 • Open 9am–6pm • Closed Dec 25 • Adm • www.aquariumofpacific.org*

Museum of Latin American Art (MOLAA)

7 Part of Long Beach's emerging East Village Arts District, this lively museum is the only one in the western United States dedicated to showcasing the work of artists who've lived or worked in Latin America since 1945. The collection offers great insight into the culture and concerns of artists from Mexico to Tierra del Fuego and every country in between. The restaurant is a lovely spot for lunch. ◈ *Map E6 • 628 Alamitos Ave, Long Beach • 562-437-1689 • Open 11:30am–7pm Tue–Fri, 11am–7pm Sat, 11am–6pm Sun • Adm (free Fri) • www.molaa.org*

Long Beach Museum of Art

8 This small community museum mounts several temporary exhibits annually in addition to showing selections from its permanent collection. A tour of the galleries yields encounters with paintings and drawings by early 20th-century European and Californian artists along with furniture and decorative objects from throughout American history. The museum is

Log on to www.aquariumofthepacific.org for more information on the Aquarium of the Pacific

Cactus Garden in Rancho Los Alamitos

distinguished by a waterfront location with great views of Long Beach's famous offshore oil wells. ◈ Map F6 • 2300 E Ocean Blvd • 562-439-2119 • Open 11am–5pm Tue–Sun • Adm • www.lbma.org

9 Naples & Belmont Shore

Naples is an Italian-flavored peninsula in Alamitos Bay, which is connected by a causeway to Belmont Shore with its many shopping and dining options. Long Beach's poshest neighborhood, Naples was dreamed up by Arthur Parsons in 1903, around the same time Abbott Kinney conceived of Venice (see p118). Enjoy an authentic Venetian gondola ride (see p138). ◈ Map F6 • Southern Long Beach

10 Ranchos Los Alamitos & Los Cerritos

In 1784, Manuel Nieto, a corporal in the Spanish army, was granted 300,000 acres of land in recognition of his services. The land was later divided into five ranchos, including Rancho Los Alamitos and Rancho Los Cerritos. The ranch houses are some of the state's oldest structures. ◈ Map F6 • Rancho Los Alamitos, 6400 Bixby Hill Rd, 562-431-3541, Free • Rancho Los Cerritos, 4600 Virginia Rd, 562-570-1755, Free

A Day of Maritime Meandering

Morning

Begin your day at the **Los Angeles Maritime Museum** in San Pedro where you'll find interesting nuggets of information about the city's nautical heritage. A short stroll north through the little park takes you to a modern fire station building at the bottom of 5th Street. It houses a still functional 1925 fire boat capable of pumping over 10,000 gallons (45,000 liters) of water a minute. Historic boat buffs could continue north another half mile (800 m) for a tour of the **SS** *Lane Victory* at Berth 94, an immaculately restored WWII cargo ship.

Backtrack on foot or take the electric trolley to **Ports O' Call Village** to browse the souvenir shops and have lunch.

Afternoon

Once fortified, join a one-hour narrated cruise for close-ups of the amazing operations of the **Los Angeles Harbor**, the nation's largest.

Head back to your car and drive south on Harbor Boulevard to Pacific Avenue, then left to get to the **Cabrillo Marine Aquarium** for a look at aquatic life in California's waters. For great sunset views, head west on Shepard Street, then north on South Gaffey Street to the bluff-top **Angels Gate Park**. A nice feature here is the Korean Friendship Bell, a replica of an 8th-century original built for a Korean king. Conclude the day with dinner in Pine Avenue in **Long Beach**.

Left **Observation Bar** Right **Wheelhouse**

Features of the Queen Mary

1 Ghost & Legends Tour
This special effects walking tour is hokey and takes you deep into the ship's bowels, including the vast boiler room and the First Class Swimming Pool.

2 First Class Swimming Pool
The large lavish pool was once filled with salt water but is empty now and said to be a vortex of ghostly activity.

3 Observation Bar
Visit this Art Deco masterpiece of sparkling chrome and polished hardwood for the carved and curved balustrade and mural painting behind the bar.

4 Engine Room
One of the fastest ocean liners of its time, the *Queen Mary* had a cruising speed of 28.5 knots (34 mph or 55 km/h) and was driven by four steam turbine engines each turning its own propeller.

5 Wheelhouse
Located above the deck officers' quarters, the wheelhouse was the navigational control center of the ship. It features dual brass steering wheels and such modern communication equipment as the "loudaphone," an onboard telephone system.

6 Promenade Deck
This deck held most of the First Class common areas as well as the wonderful wooden outdoor walkway, now worn.

7 Queen's Salon
First Class passengers once enjoyed dances, concerts, and religious services in the Promenade Deck grand hall. It is now used for special events.

Detail inside the Queen's Salon

8 Champagne Sunday Brunch
Pick your favorites from 11 culinary stations serving everything from roast beef to salads while a harpist serenades you. It's all set up in the glorious Grand Salon, the original First Class dining room. Reservations are recommended.

9 Sir Winston's
This silver service restaurant was named in honor of the famous British Prime Minister Winston Churchill. During World War II, he traveled to three conferences in the United States aboard the *Queen Mary*.

10 Scorpion
This original Soviet submarine, moored right next to the *Queen Mary*, saw service from 1973 to 1994. A self-guided tour takes in the engine room, the kitchen, and other cramped quarters. ◈ *10am–6pm • Adm*

L'Opera

Price Categories

Price categories include a three-course meal for one, a glass of house wine, and all unavoidable extra charges including tax.

$	under $25
$$	$25–$50
$$$	$50–$80
$$$$	over $80

🔟 Places to Eat

1 L'Opera
A lofty ceiling supported by marble columns provides a wonderfully theatrical setting for tasty fettucine, *frutti di mare*, and *veal scallopine*. ◎ *Map E6 • 101 Pine Ave • 562-491-0066 • $$$*

2 Alegria Cocina Latina
Spanish and Latin American food and a hip crowd make it a popular bistro. Live entertainment on weekends. ◎ *Map E6 • 115 Pine Ave • 562-436-3388 • $*

3 The Madison
The cathedral ceiling and decor of a 1920s bank building provide an elegant backdrop for American fare. Try the perfect prime steaks. ◎ *Map E6 • 102 Pine Ave • 562-628-8866 • $$$*

4 Yard House
This pub crawlers' haunt has almost 200 international brews from on tap, from Budweiser to obscure drafts such as Saxer Lemon Lager. ◎ *Map E6 • 401 Shoreline Village Dr • 562-628-0455 • $$*

5 Tequila Jack's
This cantina serves good Mexican food. Try the marvellous tequila straight or blended with a margarita. On Tuesdays tacos are only a dollar. ◎ *Map E6 • 407 Shoreline Village Dr • 562-628-0454 • $$*

6 Parker's Lighthouse
Great views of the *Queen Mary* are among the perks of dining at this fish restaurant. The big combination platters are the way to go. ◎ *Map E6 • 435 Shoreline Village Dr • 562-432-6500 • $*

7 Sir Winston's
Fancy yourself royalty when dining at this old-fashioned romantic restaurant aboard the *Queen Mary*. The *beef phyllo* is recommended. Dress code. ◎ *Map E6 • 1126 Queens Highway • 562-435-3511 • $$*

8 The Reef
Great views of the Long Beach skyline coupled with delicious fresh fish and seafood. The four-course Sunset Dinner special is a steal. ◎ *Map E6 • 880 Harbor Scenic Dr • 562-435-8013 • $*

9 Belmont Brewing Co
The tables on the huge deck overlooking the Belmont Pier are the most coveted. Wash down the tasty pizza with the home-made beers. ◎ *Map F6 • 25 39th Place, Belmont Shore • 562-433-3891 • $*

10 Sushi of Naples
You'll love the sushi and teriyaki chicken. Special combos at lunch and discounted specials at night. ◎ *Map F6 • 5470 E 2nd St, Belmont Shore • 562-434-1122 • $$*

Unless otherwise stated, all restaurants accept credit cards, serve vegetarian meals, and provide access for the disabled

131

STREETSMART

LOS ANGELES TOP 10

Left **Redondo Beach** Center **Packing right** Right **Distances in miles**

🔟 Planning your Trip

1 When to Go
The chief tourist season in LA is in July and August when the beaches are fairly pleasant though inland areas can get uncomfortably hot and smoggy. Another good time to visit Los Angeles is in winter, which brings less smog, smaller crowds, and plummeting hotel prices.

2 Weather
LA has a moderate climate with low humidity and cool evenings, even in summer. Rain is most likely from January to March. Summers are sunny and pleasant.

3 What to Pack
Californians dress casually, but LA can be chilly in winter, and even in summer you'll need a jacket or sweater in the evenings, especially near the coast. Sunglasses and hats are must-haves, and are easily available anywhere in LA.

4 Where to Stay
Los Angeles is huge and offers a wide variety of accomodations. Santa Monica is the most visitor-friendly of the beach towns. Beverly Hills is for the wealthy, while downtown and Pasadena are great places to stay for culture-vultures and architecture fans. Urban types should opt for the hip and happening Hollywood or West Hollywood.

5 Travel Insurance
Most US insurance is effective throughout the country, but those with foreign insurance coverage should take out comprehensive travel insurance before arriving in the US. Most insurance plans include luggage theft or loss, but what is most crucial is that they should cover medical emergencies.

6 Passports & Visas
Citizens of the UK, Canada, Australia, New Zealand, Ireland, and several other countries – mostly European – need a valid machine-readable passport to visit the US for a period of up to 90 days. If you arrive by air or sea, you must present a round-trip ticket. Nationals of all other countries require a visa. Regulations may change, so check with a US consulate or the US State Department's websites.

7 Electricity
The US has 115-120V current, rather than the 220V current used in other countries. Plugs are of the two-prong variety. Appliances that are not compatible with this electrical system require a transformer and/or an adapter.

8 Measurements
Unlike most other nations, the US does not use the metric system. Weight is measured in ounces, pounds, and tons; distances in inches, feet, yards, and miles; and temperature in Fahrenheit. Carry a pocket converter or conversion chart for convenience.

9 Time
LA is in the Pacific Time Zone, which is eight hours behind GMT – when it's midnight in LA it's 3am the next day in New York, 8am in the UK, 9am in Central Europe, and 6pm in Australia and New Zealand.

10 Children's Needs
If traveling with children, book into child-friendly accommodations – at many hotels kids can stay for free in their parents' room (see p149). If you need someone to watch over the tots, ask the concierge. Most attractions and museums discount admission for children, though age requirements may vary.

Websites

US State Department
www.travel.state.gov/visa_services.html

Los Angeles Convention & Visitors Bureau
www.lacvb.com

Los Angeles Times
www.latimes.com

LA Weekly
www.laweekly.com

Left **Tipping a waiter** Right **LA listings publications**

🔟 General Information

1 Tipping
In restaurants a tip of 15 to 20 percent is standard. An easy way to figure out the amount is by doubling the sales tax shown on your bill. Cab drivers, masseurs, hairdressers, and other service personnel expect about 10 to 15 percent.

2 Taxes
The current sales tax in LA is about 8.25 percent. It must be added to all restaurant bills, and non-food items such as clothing, alcohol, and suntan lotion; it is included in gasoline prices, theater tickets, and museum admissions. Services are not taxable. Hotel rooms are subject to an occupancy tax which varies slightly within Los Angeles, from 12 percent in Santa Monica to 14 percent in Beverly Hills.

3 Tourist Offices
LA Inc, the city's visitors bureau, operates two visitor information centers. In addition, cities such as Santa Monica and Beverly Hills have their own offices.

4 Entertainment Listings
A great source for events listings is the *Los Angeles Times* daily Calendar section; the *LA Weekly*, a freebie available across town, also provides good "what's-on" information.

5 International Publications
Foreign and out-of-town newspapers and periodicals may be found at the airport, in bookstores such as Barnes & Noble, as well as at specialty newsstands around LA.

6 Television
All the major TV networks have studios in Los Angeles, including KNBC (Channel 4) and FOX (Channel 11). WB (Warner Bros, Channel 5) and UPN (Channel 13) are smaller networks, while KCAL (Channel 9) is a local station.

7 Radio
Numerous radio stations crowd the LA air waves – Arrow 93 (93.1FM) features rock oldies, The Wave (94.7FM) offers smooth jazz, KISS (102.7FM) plays Top 40 chart music, and K-Mozart (105.1FM) presents classical sounds. KCRW (89.9F) is LA's main affiliate of NPR (National Public Radio).

8 Public Holidays
Banks, offices, and some museums are closed on these national holidays – Jan 1, Martin Luther King Jr. Day (3rd Mon in Jan), Presidents' Day (3rd Mon in Feb), Memorial Day (last Mon in May), Independence Day (Jul 4), Labor Day (1st Mon in Sep), Columbus Day (2nd Mon in Oct), Veterans' Day (Nov 11), Thanksgiving (4th Thu in Nov), and Christmas Day (Dec 25).

9 Opening Hours
Stores in shopping malls and streets are usually open from 10am to 9pm Monday to Saturday, and to 6pm on Sunday. Banks are closed on weekends, but ATMs are accessible 24/7.

10 Discounts
Students, seniors, and children usually qualify for reduced admission at museums and attractions. Proof of age or status may be required.

Directory

Consulates
• UK: 11766 Wilshire Blvd, 310-481-0031
• Canada: 550 S Hope St, 213-346-2700
• Australia: 2049 Century Park East, 310-229-4800 • New Zealand: 12400 Wilshire Blvd, 310-207-1605
• All Other Consulates: Call 411

Visitors Centers
• Downtown: 213-689-8822 • Santa Monica: 310-393-7593
• Beverly Hills: 310-248-1015

Area Codes
• Downtown: 213
• Hollywood: 323
• Pasadena: 626
• Beverly Hills, Westwood, Santa Monica: 310 • Long Beach: 562

Streetsmart

For information on transportation in LA See p137

Left **Los Angeles International Airport (LAX)** Right **LA shuttle**

⑩ Arriving in Los Angeles

1 Arriving by Air
International and national flights land at Los Angeles International Airport (LAX), while smaller airports in Burbank, Ontario, Irvine, and Long Beach serve only domestic flights.

2 Customs
Travelers arriving in the US are permitted to import one liter of liquor, 200 cigarettes (or 50 cigars), and $100 worth of gifts ($400 for US or permanent residents) without incurring customs fees. No meat, seeds, plants, or fresh fruit may be brought in.

3 Immigration
Anyone arriving in the US must complete one customs declaration per household and, in the case of non-citizens, immigration form I-94. Strict security checks, involving the taking of photographs and fingerprints, are now in place for those arriving in the US on a visa.

4 Los Angeles International Airport (LAX)
LAX occupies a vast ocean-adjacent plot of land about 5 miles (8 km) south of Santa Monica and 16 miles (25 km) southwest of downtown and Hollywood. The free Shuttle A bus frequently connects each of the eight terminals, including the Tom Bradley International Terminal.

5 Shuttles
Several shuttle buses stop outside each terminal on the lower level of LAX. Door-to-door van shuttles are usually more economical than taxis but are also more time-consuming. Most airport area hotels operate a free pick-up service.

6 Taxis
Taxis must be summoned by a dispatcher waiting outside each terminal on the arrival level. Fares vary but range from $20–35, to Santa Monica, downtown, and Hollywood. Note that an airport surcharge applies to all trips originating from LAX.

7 Other LA Area Airports
Domestic travelers might be able to obtain cheaper fares for flights to regional LA airports, which are also smaller and less busy than LAX. Burbank is close to downtown, Pasadena, and the major movie studios. Airports in Long Beach and Irvine are convenient if you are headed for Disneyland.

8 Arriving by Train
Amtrak trains arriving at the historic Union Station in downtown include the Coast Starlight from Seattle, the Southwest Chief from Chicago, and the Sunset Limited from Orlando. The Pacific Surf-liner that travels between San Diego and San Luis Obispo also stops here.

9 Arriving by Bus
Greyhound operates a vast network of air-conditioned coaches all across the US. Bus travel is cheapest but is much slower and a suitable option only if you're arriving from nearby cities such as San Francisco or Las Vegas. Buses stop at the main Greyhound terminal in an industrial section of downtown, an area best avoided after dark.

10 Arriving by Car
Several freeways lead straight to and through LA, including the I-5, Hwy 101, and I-405 from points north; the I-10 from the east; and the I-5 and I-405 from the south.

Directory

Airports
• LAX: 310-646-5252, www.lawa.org

Shuttles
• Xpress Shuttle: 800-427-7483 • Prime Time: 800-473-3743

Train
• Union Station: 800 N Alameda St • Amtrak: 800-872-7245, www.amtrak.com

Bus
• Greyhound: 800-229-9424, www.greyhound.com

Note: Sharp objects such as corkscrews cannot be carried as part of hand luggage while arriving or departing from the US

Left **LA taxi** Center **Metro Rapid bus** Right **Metro on Red Line**

Getting Around Los Angeles

1 Car Rentals
Unlike other major cities, a car is essential to getting around LA quickly because of the great distances involved. Rentals require a credit card and driver's license.

2 Rental Insurance
US insurance policies generally cover rental cars as well, while foreign ones almost never do. Check with your insurer for details. Some credit cards may provide secondary coverage if used to pay for the rental.

3 Parking
Free street parking is available in most neighborhoods, although it pays to study the posted restrictions. Stopping or parking is not allowed at red curbs. Some cities, including Santa Monica and Beverly Hills, have inexpensive city-run parking lots. Valet parking is common at restaurants and the better hotels.

4 Driving in LA
By and large, LA is relatively easy to navigate. Wearing a seatbelt, even in the backseat, is compulsory. Unless posted otherwise, the speed limit is 35 mph (56 km/h) on city streets and 55 mph (89 km/h) on freeways. Turning right on a red light at intersections is legal unless otherwise posted.

5 Maps
Locals swear by the book-sized Thomas Guide, but a general street map should suffice for getting around. You'll find these at gas stations or convenience stores, although the most current ones are those published by the American Automobile Association (AAA).

6 Taxis
Getting around town by taxi can be a pricey proposition unless you're traveling as a group or are only going a short distance. Taxi drivers usually won't respond to being hailed but must be ordered in advance.

7 Public Transportation
Getting around LA using public transportation is best reserved for short distances or cross-town travel. The network consists of buses, light rail lines, and a subway line, most of which are operated by the Metropolitan Transportation Authority (MTA).

8 Buses
The downtown DASH buses and the Big Blue Bus in Santa Monica/Venice/Westwood offer good service. For a cheap mini tour, take MTA's express Metro Rapid No. 720 from Santa Monica to downtown along Wilshire Boulevard through Beverly Hills.

9 Light Rail & Subway
MTA operates three light rail lines – the Blue Line from downtown to Long Beach, the Green Line from Redondo Beach to Norwalk, and the brand-new Gold Line from downtown to Pasadena. MTA's Red Line, LA's only subway route, goes from downtown to Universal City through Hollywood.

10 Walking
"Nobody walks in LA," as the song goes, and this is largely true. However, some areas are more conducive to walking, such as the crowded downtown or the fun Melrose Avenue and Venice Boardwalk.

Directory

Car Rentals
• Avis: 800-831-2847
• Enterprise: 800-736-8222 • Hertz: 800-654-3131 • National: 800-328-4567

Maps
• AAA: 800-874-7532 (for members only)

Taxis
• Checkers: 800-300-5007 • Yellow Cab: 800-200-1085

Public Transportation
• MTA: 800-266-6883

Buses
• Big Blue Bus: 310-451-5444
• DASH: 310-808-2273

Left **Red Line Tours** Center **Cruise tour** Right **The Santa Catalina Island Co. Discovery Tours sign**

📖10 Guided Tours

1 Red Line Tours
During these daily walking tours led by knowledgeable guides, you are made to wear special audio-systems to cut out traffic noise. Catch up on Hollywood history, and learn about the grand old days of downtown and its exciting new architecture.

2 LA Conservancy Tours
The LA Conservancy conducts wonderful architecture-themed guided walking tours of downtown every Saturday morning.

3 Neon Cruise
For an "illuminating" look at LA, join the night tour organized by the Museum of Neon Art (see p76), which takes you through neon signs, both historic and contemporary, and sparkling movie marquees.

4 Boat Tours
Fisherman's Village in Marina del Rey, San Pedro's Ports O' Call Village, and Shoreline Village in Long Beach are all departure points for various boat cruises, including spins around the harbors and whale-watching trips.

5 Gondola Getaway
Sample the pleasures of the canals of Long Beach's Naples neighborhood aboard an authentic Venetian gondola.

6 Starline Tours
This company offers classic narrated bus tours of LA, including the popular two-hour Movie Stars' Homes Tour and the 5 1/2-hour Grand Tour of Los Angeles. Tours depart continuously throughout the day.

7 LA Bike Tours
Exploring LA from the saddle is a great way to see the city while staying fit. The guided and narrated tours focus on specific neighborhoods but rides in the Santa Monica Mountains can also be organized.

8 Santa Catalina Island Company Discovery Tours
This company organizes several land- and sea-based excursions lasting from one to four hours. Options include a glass-bottom boat tour and the excellent Island Tour.

9 Art Museum Tours
LACMA in midtown (see pp16–19) offers up to five different gallery talks daily. The Getty (see pp12–15) also runs daily art, architecture, and garden tours.

10 Take My Mother Please
Personal tour guide Anne Block custom-designs tours of LA – you'll be chauffeured in great style to bars, cafés, clubs, museums, or whatever else takes your fancy.

Directory

Red Line Tours
• Hollywood: 6773 Hollywood Blvd
• Downtown: 304 S Broadway, 323-402-1074

LA Conservancy Tours
• 213-623-2489, www. laconservancy.org

Neon Cruise
• MONA: 213-489-9918, www.neon mona.org/cruise

Boat Tours
• Hornblower Cruises: 13755 Fiji Way, Marina del Rey; 310-301-6000
• Spirit Cruises: 429 Shoreline Village Dr, 310-548-8080
• Los Angeles Harbor Cruises: Ports O' Call, Berth 78, San Pedro; 310-831-0996

Gondola Getaway
• 5437 E Ocean Blvd, 562-433-9595, www.gondo.net

Starline Tours
• 800-959-3131, www.starlinetours. com

LA Bike Tours
6731 Hollywood Blvd, 323-466-5890

Santa Catalina Island Company Discovery Tours
800-626-1496

Take My Mother Please
323-737-2200, www.takemymother please.com

Rush-hour traffic

Things to Avoid

1 Rush-hour Traffic
Heavy traffic is one of LA's major drawbacks. To prevent being stuck in a traffic jam, especially on freeways, avoid traveling from 7 to 9am and 4 to 7pm on week days. Traffic is also heavy on Sunday afternoons and at the beginning and end of holiday periods.

2 Crime-prone Areas
Visitors to LA rarely fall victim to attacks on person or property. Most areas are perfectly safe for walking around, especially during the day. Keep your wits about you in east LA and south-central LA, and stay away altogether from these neighborhoods after dark. The streets of Hollywood and Venice, and beaches and parks are also dodgy after sundown.

3 Summer Crowds
During the main tourist season in July and August, crowds at major attractions often swell to capacity, especially at big theme parks such as Disneyland and Universal Studios, where two-hour waits for three-minute rides are common. Remember to pack water and plenty of patience.

4 Ocean Pollution
LA's ocean waters may not be as pristine as those of Polynesia, but they are clean enough for frolicking in the surf at most times. The major exception is after rainy days when garbage flushes straight from the storm drains into the ocean, dangerously raising pollution levels. Swimming is prohibited for three days after the rains have stopped.

5 June Gloom
This pesky weather phenomenon arrives almost like clockwork in late spring, cloaking the entire city in a thick layer of fog and clouds that last days and weeks at a time. Visitors drawn to LA by the legendary California sunshine and the laid-back summer lifestyle should avoid the city during this month.

6 Sightseeing Excesses
LA novice visitors sometimes make the mistake of packing too much sightseeing into a single day, which can be exhausting. Don't underestimate the time it takes to travel between attractions or the tiring summer heat. If limited time is a factor, join an organized tour or focus your explorations on a single neighborhood.

7 Traveling during Major Holidays
Higher costs, packed planes and airports, frayed nerves, and crowded attractions are among the main factors that make travel during major holidays (see p135) a stressful affair. Avoid scheduling your trip around Memorial Day, July 4, Labor Day, Thanksgiving, Christmas, and New Year's Day.

8 Road Rage
As if LA's heavy traffic wasn't bad enough, many people tend to adopt an unpleasant and aggressive attitude behind the wheel. Sudden lane changes right in front of you, not allowing you to change lanes, or driving right behind you are just some of the antics. Keep your cool and don't allow the situation to escalate. In case the situation worsens, make sure your car doors are locked.

9 Going Topless
Compared to most European nations, America is, overall, a rather prudish country. Dropping your bikini top on the beach will not only generate unwelcome stares but quite possibly, a fine as well. Most restaurants, even casual ones located on the beach, require a minimum of shorts, a t-shirt, and shoes.

10 Public Drinking
Drinking on the sidewalk, the beach, in a park, or any other public space is prohibited by law, and you will be fined if caught.

Left **City Pass** Center **A hostel sign** Right **Fleamarket at Melrose Trading Post**

Los Angeles on a Budget

1 Free Sightseeing
Some of the best things to see and do in Los Angeles don't cost a cent – bumming around in the beach, strolling down the Venice Boardwalk, hiking up the Santa Monica Mountains, touring the Getty Center, or listening to street musicians on the Third Street Promenade are some fantastic options.

2 Museums
Some of LA's finest museums, including the Getty Center, the California Science Center, and the California African American Museum, do not charge admission. Many others offer free entry once a week or once a month *(see individual listings in this book for more details)*.

3 City Pass Hollywood
If you're planning to immerse yourself in Hollywood glamour, City Pass buys admission to five major attractions and tours for a nominal sum. This currently includes Universal Studios, the Autry Museum of Western Heritage, the Hollywood Entertainment Museum, Starline Bus Tours, and Kodak Theatre.

4 Free Events
Summer is a great time for free outdoor concerts and events. Venues hosting regular performances include the Santa Monica Pier, the Getty Center, the Skirball Center, and the Water Court near MOCA. Free festivals celebrating LA's multicultural tapestry take place all year.

5 Free TV Shows
Watch your favorite TV stars in action by attending a live taping at a major studio. Free tickets are available through Audiences Unlimited or from studio audience scouts in places such as the Venice Boardwalk or the Farmers Markets.

6 Lodging
While hostels are great for gregarious types, chain motels are best for budget travelers in need of privacy. Some motels and hotels offer American Automobile Association members and its affiliates a discount. Bargaining is possible during the slack tourist season. Look for coupon magazines available at gas stations and tourist offices.

7 Shopping
Bargains abound in LA, with department stores and boutiques mounting special sales year-round, especially around public holidays. For extra savings, look for coupons in the Sunday *Los Angeles Times*. Flea markets, vintage stores, and thrift shops offer unique finds at cut-throat prices.

8 Restaurants
Tanking up for little money is very easy in LA. Fast-food and chain restaurants are ubiquitous, of course, but it's also possible to eat cheaply at better restaurants. Go for lunch instead of dinner, avoid ordering alcoholic drinks, and take advantage of promotions or "early bird" specials served before the dinner rush.

9 Happy Hours
A fun way to wind down the day, Happy Hours are usually held on weekdays between 5pm and 7pm, though precise hours may vary. Most eateries also offer free snacks or a discounted appetizer menu.

10 Theater Tickets
There's plenty of live theater in LA, but tickets can be expensive. Half-price tickets for selected plays are available on the Internet through the popular Theatre LA.

Directory

Free Events
• City of Los Angeles Cultural Affairs Dept: 213-473-7700, www. culturela.org

Free TV Shows
• Audiences Unlimited: 818-753-3470

Theater Tickets
• Theatre LA: www.theatrela.org

Left **Automated Teller Machine (ATM)** Center **Phone card** Right **US Mail van**

TOP 10 Banking & Communications

1 Banking Hours
Most banks are open from Monday through Friday, usually from 9am or 10am to 6pm, though a few branches also do business on Saturday until 1pm or 2pm. Branches of Wells Fargo, Bank of America, and Washington Mutual can be found all across LA.

2 ATMs
Automated Teller Machines (ATMs) are found at almost all banks and are open 24 hours a day. Most are equipped to handle transactions using bank and credit cards linked to one of the worldwide networks, such as Star, Plus, or Cirrus. A small fee is usually required.

3 Credit Cards
A credit card is a very common form of payment in the US, with nearly universal acceptance of MasterCard and Visa and, to a lesser extent, American Express and JCB. Cash advances from ATMs using credit cards mostly start accruing interest immediately.

4 Traveler's Checks
Traveler's checks in US dollars are widely accepted in restaurants, supermarkets, banks, and stores; personal checks on an out-of-state (outside California) or foreign account are not. Practically all banks cash traveler's checks for a

fee; American Express offices encash their company-issued checks for free. Bring a passport or some form of ID.

5 Public Pay Phones
Public telephones can be found on city streets throughout LA, as well as in gas stations, libraries, shopping malls, beaches, and many other places. Phones only accept coins, which can be a hassle when making long-distance calls. Many pay phones accept incoming calls as well.

6 Phone Cards
Prepaid phone cards eliminate the need for coins at pay phones and may also help save on calls placed from hotels. Available in many supermarkets, gas stations, and electronics stores in amounts starting at $5, they require you to dial a toll-free access number before making your call. Read the small print as some of the less respectable ones come with extra charges on top of the per minute rate.

7 Post Office Hours
General post office hours are 8am to 5pm Monday to Friday and 8am to 2pm Saturday, though timings may vary slightly from branch to branch. For specifics and branch locations, call 800-275-8777. Stamps are easily available in supermarkets too.

8 Sending Mail
Postage for letters sent within the US costs 37 cents for the first ounce and 23 cents for each additional ounce; a postcard stamp is 23 cents. One-ounce airmail letters cost 80 cents and postcards 70 cents.

9 Express & Courier Mail
The US Postal Service (USPS) offers overnight service within the US, and global two- to three-day delivery. FedEx and UPS are the dominant private courier services.

10 Internet Access
Many hotels now have free data port connections for laptop Net access. Computer terminals are available, mostly in upscale hotels. Wireless terminals that allow you to go online through the in-room TV are also common. Libraries or Internet cafés also offer access to the Internet.

Directory

Express & Courier Mail
- USPS: 800-222-1811
- FedEx: 800-247-4747
- UPS: 800-742-5877

Internet Cafés
- Cyber Java: 7080 Hollywood Blvd, 323-466-5600
- Cyber HQ: 4682 Eagle Rock Blvd, 323-257-3600

Left **Ambulance** Center **Sign for a 24-hour pharmacy** Right **Pharmacy store**

Security & Health

1 Emergency Numbers
Dial 911 for any kind of emergency (ambulance, police, fire, etc). A toll-free number, it will be answered by an operator who will send out the respective emergency response service.

2 Medical Assistance
In a serious emergency, medical assistance is available 24 hours a day in hospital emergency rooms. Cheaper alternatives are urgent care clinics, which accept patients on a walk-in basis. Call your insurance company for a referral to a local doctor or check the Yellow Pages in case of non-emergencies.

3 Free & Low-cost Clinics
If traveling without insurance, you can keep medical costs low by visiting a subsidized clinic.

4 Pharmacies
Major drugstore chains such as Sav-on, Longs Drugs, and Rite Aid contain full-service pharmacies, most of which keep late hours (many remain open 24 hours a day). If you take prescription drugs, it's best to bring along your own supply.

5 Health Insurance
Most US policies are effective throughout the country, but those with foreign insurance coverage should take out medical insurance before arriving in the US, where healthcare costs tend to be astronomical.

6 Sun Protection
Lathering up with sunscreen is essential in the fierce California sunshine unless you want to walk around with the complexion of a boiled lobster. Remember that UVA and UVB rays can do their damage even in cloudy weather.

7 Water Quality
LA tap water is heavily chlorinated and not particularly tasty despite being perfectly drinkable. Most people prefer bottled water, which is widely available. Free water served in restaurants is always tap water. The water quality in Santa Monica Bay has improved significantly in the last decade, making swimming in the ocean safe in most places, except after rainstorms when pollution levels rise temporarily (see p139).

8 Smoking
Lighting up is illegal in most public places, including airports, post offices, stores, theaters, as well as in all restaurants and cafés, though some allow smoking at outdoor tables. Some bars and nightclubs have separate outdoor patios and lounges for smoking.

9 Safety
Despite a reputation to the contrary, Los Angeles is a fairly safe city, especially in neighborhoods with the greatest appeal for tourists. Of course, common sense applies – be aware of your surroundings when using the ATM, watch your purse or wallet in crowded areas, and remember to lock your hotel room before leaving (see p139).

10 Theft
Having personal property stolen is the most likely crime you might encounter in LA. As a general rule, be wary of pickpockets in crowded areas, keep valuables locked in the hotel safe or carry them close to your body, and remember not to leave items visible in your car.

Directory

Emergency Numbers
• Travelers Aid: 310-646-2270 • Crisis Hotline: 310-392-8381

Free & Low-cost Clinics
• Venice Family Clinic: 604 Rose Ave, 310-392-8636 • LA Free Clinic: 6043 Hollywood Blvd, 8405 Beverly Blvd, 5205 Melrose Ave

Pharmacies
• 24-hour Pharmacy: 888-443-5701

Left **Disabled parking sign** Center **Ramp for wheelchair** Right **Traveling with children**

🔟 Special Needs

1 Disabled Travelers
Los Angeles is a relatively accessible town for those with visual, mobility, or hearing impairments. Most public buildings, museums, and restaurants have ramps and special bathrooms for the wheelchair-bound. Curbs are cut to facilitate movement, hotels have rooms with extra wide doors, and car rental agencies offer special hand-controlled cars.

2 Public Transportation for the Disabled
Nearly all buses and railway cars operated by MTA, LA's main public transportation agency, are accessible to people in wheelchairs. Buses are equipped with wheelchair lifts and all Metro Rail stations have walkways, ramps, or elevators. Access Services Incorporated also provides transportation for disabled people.

3 Senior Citizens
Almost all museums and attractions in Los Angeles offer discounted admission to senior citizens, though age limits at which these kick in range from 50 to 65. Airlines, Amtrak trains, and Greyhound buses may also offer reduced rates. Members of the American Association of Retired Persons (AARP) qualify for certain additional benefits.

4 Women Travelers
LA is a cosmopolitan city, and women travelers should not have any special problems. Gaining admission to trendy nightclubs is much easier for women than for men.

5 Gay & Lesbian Travelers
LA has a large gay and lesbian community, which is centered in West Hollywood; Santa Monica Boulevard, especially, is packed with happening bars, restaurants, and fitness clubs.

6 Resources for Gays & Lesbians
The LA Gay and Lesbian Center is the main local advocacy group, which also offers counseling and confidential AIDS tests. Free magazines are available in bars, eateries, and bookshops.

7 Student Travelers
LA doesn't really have a dedicated "Latin Quarter," though Westwood Village, next to UCLA, probably comes closest. Most of the beach towns have serious party scenes, especially Venice and Hermosa Beach. STA Travel, a student-oriented travel agency, has several branches in town.

8 Tips for Student Travelers
Always carry your student ID to qualify for a wide range of discounts, from transportation to movie tickets. Foreign students should carry an International Student Identity Card (ISIC).

9 Traveling with Children
Shopping malls, public restrooms, restaurants, and departmental stores have diaper-changing stations. Most restaurants have highchairs.

10 Dietary Concerns
Vegetarians, vegans, weight-watchers, or anybody else in need of a special diet will be well catered to in LA. Even if restaurant menus don't feature the required, chefs usually accommodate most preferences.

Directory

Public Transportation for the Disabled
• MTA hotline: 800-621-7828 • Access Services Inc: 800-827-0829

Senior Citizens
• AARP: 888-687-2277, www.aarp.org

Resources for Gays & Lesbians
• A Different Light Bookstore: 8853 Santa Monica Blvd • Sisterhood Bookstore: 1351 Westwood Blvd

Student Travelers
• STA Travel: 920 Westwood Blvd, 7202 Melrose Ave, 411 Santa Monica Blvd

Left **The Four Seasons** Center **The Regent Beverly Wilshire** Right **Hotel Bel-Air**

Bastions of Luxury

1 Millennium Biltmore

Baronial public areas, a Roman-style indoor pool, and a celebrity guest list characterize this grand downtown hotel. Rooms, decked in gold and blue, are warmly furnished. Afternoon tea in the Rendezvous Court and cocktails in the Gallery Bar are time-honored traditions. ✪ *Map U5 • 506 S Grand Ave • 213-624-1011 • $$$ • www.millennium-hotels.com*

2 The Four Seasons

Enormous floral arrangements welcome guests to this refined hotel whose delights include a full-service spa and free limousine rides within a 2-mile (3-km) radius. At the Windows Lounge you may find yourself sipping cocktails next to someone famous. Children under 18 stay free with parents. ✪ *Map K5 • 300 S Doheny Dr • 310-273-2222 • $$$$$ • www.fourseasons.com*

3 The Regent Beverly Wilshire

Overlooking Rodeo Drive, this dignified 1928 hotel has hosted royalty many times and featured prominently in the 1990 movie *Pretty Woman*. Luxurious extras include chauffeured car service within a radius of 3 miles (5 km). ✪ *Map C2 • 9500 Wilshire Blvd • 310-275-5200 • $$$$$ • www.regenthotels.com*

4 Hotel Bel-Air

Luxury is taken very seriously at this romantic retreat cherished for its tranquility and tropical gardens complete with white swans. Savor elegant Franco-California cuisine or sip a glass of port by a crackling fire in the piano bar. ✪ *Map C2 • 701 Stone Canyon Rd • 310-472-1211 • $$$$$ • www.hotelbelair.com*

5 The Peninsula

Antiques and artwork grace rooms, suites, and villas, all brimming with high-tech features, including wireless web access and satellite TV. A personal room valet attends to your every need. ✪ *Map C2 • 9882 S Santa Monica Blvd • 310-551-2888 • $$$$$ • www.peninsula.com*

6 Raffles L'Ermitage

Discretion is key at this sophisticated Beverly Hills hideaway with the full range of in-room high-tech amenities. Enjoy panoramic views from the rooftop pool flanked by cabanas for extra privacy. Even pets get the royal treatment. ✪ *Map K5 • 9291 Burton Way • 310-278-3344 • $$$$$ • www.raffles-lermitagehotel.com*

7 Hotel Oceana

One of Santa Monica's prettiest hotels, the Oceana has flirtatiously colorful decor reminiscent of the French Riviera. Many of the large suites have views of the ocean. ✪ *Map C3 • 849 Ocean Ave • 310-393-0486 • $$$$ • www.hoteloceana.com*

8 The Fairmont Miramar

On the site of the private home of Santa Monica's founder, Senator John Jones, the Miramar has welcomed guests since the roaring 1920s. For the ultimate in luxury, book a poolside garden bungalow. ✪ *Map A3 • 101 Wilshire Blvd • 310-576-7777 • $$$$ • www.fairmont.com*

9 Shutters on the Beach

This delightful hotel right by the sands of Santa Monica takes the beach cottage to new heights. Relax on fluffy mattresses, feel the cool ocean breeze, or watch the warm California sunlight filtering in through the shutters. ✪ *Map A4 • 1 Pico Blvd • 310-458-0030 • $$$$$ • www.shuttersonthebeach.com*

10 Casa del Mar

An imposing presence overlooking Santa Monica Beach, this 1926 beach club has been restored to its original grandeur. The grand, lavish lobby sets the tone for cosily decorated rooms. ✪ *Map A4 • 1910 Ocean Way • 310-581-5533 • $$$$$ • www.hotelcasadelmar.com*

  Unless otherwise stated, all hotels accept credit cards, have private bathrooms and air conditioning, and provide disabled access

Price Categories

For the cheapest standard double room per night (without breakfast), taxes, and extra charges.

$	under $100
$$	$100–$150
$$$	$150–$250
$$$$	$250–$350
$$$$$	over $350

Casa Malibu Inn

🔟 Beach Hotels

1 Malibu Beach Inn
Enjoy spectacular views of the coastline from Malibu's only luxury beachfront hotel with a red-tiled Mission-style building. All rooms have gas fireplaces and balconies, some with Jacuzzis. A free Continental breakfast buffet is served. ✪ *Map A3 • 22878 Pacific Coast Hwy • 310-456-6444 • $$$$ • www.malibubeachinn.com*

2 Casa Malibu Inn
This Mediterranean-style charmer is located on one of the most beautiful stretches of the California coast. Hit the waves from the private beach of the Casa Malibu Inn, then enjoy a delicious Continental breakfast. Some rooms have a kitchen and a cosy fireplace. ✪ *Map A3 • 22752 Pacific Coast Hwy • 310-456-2219 • No dis. access • $$*

3 Le Merigot
Centrally located, this Santa Monica hotel has the elegant personality of a Mediterranean mansion. Rooms are dressed in sunny, golden colors and feature patios, heavenly beds, and big desks. Bold chandeliers light up the Cézanne restaurant, where you can taste exquisite French cuisine. Excellent in-house spa. ✪ *Map A4 • 1740 Ocean Ave • 310-395-9700 • $$$$ • www.lemerigotbeachhotel.com*

4 Hotel California
This delightful Santa Monica cottage trades grandness for whimsy. Blonde wood furniture, hardwood floors, and hand-painted surfboards doubling as headboards add to the breezy feel. ✪ *Map B3 • 670 Ocean Ave • 310-393-2363 • Dis. access in one suite • No air conditioning • $$$ • www.hotelca.com*

5 Cadillac Hotel
Charlie Chaplin liked to spend summers in this Art Deco landmark on Venice Boardwalk, whose funkiness can be a drawback after dark. Clean but basic rooms, including some four-bed dorms. ✪ *Map A5 • 8 Dudley Ave • 310-399-8876 • No air conditioning • $ • www.thecadillachotel.com*

6 Best Western Marina Pacific Hotel & Suites
A pleasant Venice beach hotel, this gives you easy access to interesting cafés and stores. The attractive rooms come with the full range of amenities and rates include Continental breakfast. ✪ *Map A6 • 1697 Pacific Ave • 310-452-1111 • Dis. access in two rooms • $$ • www.mphotel.com*

7 Best Western Jamaica Bay Inn
For beachfront on a budget, opt for this pleasant Marina del Rey hotel right on Mother's Beach. The sand-colored rooms have private patios or balconies. ✪ *Map C3 • 4175 Admiralty Way • 310-823-5333 • No dis. access • $$ • www.bestwestern-pacifichotels.com*

8 Ritz-Carlton Marina del Rey
Overlooking the world's largest custom-built pleasure boat harbor, the Ritz-Carlton offers European elegance and deluxe creature comforts. Indulge in global cuisine at the stylish Jer-ne restaurant. ✪ *Map C3 • 4375 Admiralty Way • 310-823-1700 • $$$ • www.ritzcarlton.com*

9 Beach House at Hermosa
Within earshot of the waves, this casually elegant getaway is the perfect antidote to stress. Just relax in front of the crackling fire in your roomy suites. ✪ *Map C5 • 1300 The Strand • 310-374-3001 • $$$$ • www.beach-house.com*

10 Sea Sprite Motel
Rooms in this Hermosa Beach hotel won't win the style awards, but with a location right on the beach, you probably won't spend much time inside. Larger units sleep up to six. ✪ *Map C5 • 1016 The Strand • 310-376-6933 • No dis. access • No air conditioning • $$ • www.seaspritemotel.com*

Streetsmart

Left **Ritz-Carlton Huntington Hotel** Center **Chateau Marmont** Right **Hotel Queen Mary**

🔟 Historic Charmers

1 Figueroa Hotel
This hotel's unique personality greets you as soon you enter its soaring columned lobby with colorful tiles and exotic furnishings. The rooms offer basic comforts and a lovely color-splashed Moroccan theme. ✪ Map T5 • 939 S Figueroa St • 213-627-8971 • $$ • www.figueroahotel.com

2 Ritz-Carlton Huntington Hotel
A grand old-world style resort, this is a destination in itself. Have your breakfast alfresco and lounge by the Olympic-sized pool, followed by a pampering session in the full-service spa. Enjoy high tea in the afternoon, then hit the tennis courts before changing for dinner at the elegant restaurant. A perfect day, indeed! ✪ Map F2 • 1401 S Oak Knoll Ave • 626-568-3900 • $$$$ • www.ritzcarlton.com

3 Hollywood Roosevelt
A stone's throw away from Hollywood and Highland, this famous Hollywood hotel recently reinvented itself. While the grand lobby still pays homage to the original Spanish-Mediterranean decor, most rooms now have 21st-century amenities. Only the poolside cabanas retain an old-fashioned flair. ✪ Map P2 • 7000 Hollywood Blvd • 323-466-7000 • $$$ • www.hollywoodroosevelt.com

4 Chateau Marmont
Famous recluses such as Greta Garbo holed up in this quirky French castle-style hotel, whose policy of discretion still ensures steady celebrity bookings. Revel in Hollywood lore in the cottages, bungalows, and suites. ✪ Map M3 • 8221 W Sunset Blvd • 323-656-1010 • $$$$ • www.chateaumarmont.com

5 The Argyle
Once the home of John Wayne and mobster Bugsy Siegel, The Argyle is a striking 1929 Art Deco tower. The former apartments are now luxuriously appointed rooms and suites, with reproductions of 1920s period furniture. ✪ Map M3 • 8358 Sunset Blvd • 323-654-7100 • $$$$ • www.argylehotel.com

6 The Georgian Hotel
This 1933 seaside hotel was an instant hit with the movie elite seeking to escape the Hollywood heat. Behind the Art Deco façade await newly spiffed up guest rooms in chocolate colors, most with ocean views. ✪ Map A4 • 1415 Ocean Ave • 310-395-9945 • $$$ • www.georgianhotel.com

7 Beverly Hills Hotel
It's no longer the trendiest of LA's luxury hotels, but its exalted place in Hollywood history remains. Drinks in the Polo Lounge, tanning by the poolside, and opulent comforts are all part of the unforgettable experience. ✪ Map J4 • 9641 Sunset Blvd • 310-276-2251 • $$$$$ • www.beverlyhillshotel.com

8 Shangri-la Hotel
Dating from 1939, this hotel doesn't quite manage to combine nostalgia with modern amenities. However, its oceanfront Santa Monica location is great and the large rooms have ocean views. Rates include parking, a small breakfast, and tea. ✪ Map A3 • 1301 Ocean Ave • 310-394-2791 • $$$ • www.shangrilahotel.com

9 Hotel Queen Mary
Stay in the roomy quarters of the Queen Mary with their polished wood and thick carpets to savor the romantic ambience of a bygone era (see p130). ✪ Map E6 • 1126 Queens Hwy • 562-435-3511 • $ • www.queenmary.com

10 Zane Gray Pueblo Hotel
Built by American Western writer Zane Gray in 1926, this is a charming rustic retreat on Catalina Island with lovely views of the yacht-dotted Avalon Bay. An excellent getaway from the bustle of big city LA. ✪ Map 199 Chimes Tower Rd, Avalon • 310-510-0966 • No dis. access • No air conditioning • $$ • www.zanegraypueblohotel.com

Unless otherwise stated, all hotels accept credit cards, have private bathrooms and air conditioning, and provide disabled access

Left Mondrian **Right Maison 140**

Price Categories

For the cheapest standard double room per night (without breakfast), taxes, and extra charges.

$	under $100
$$	$100–$150
$$$	$150–$250
$$$$	$250–$350
$$$$$	over $350

🔟 Chic & Hip Hotels

1 The Standard Downtown

Downtown's first trendy hotel made an immediate splash when it debuted in 2002. The rooftop bar with its balmy pool and trendy scene is the place to be. Rooms are large with minimalist interiors. ◈ *Map U4 • 550 S Flower St • 213-892-8080 • $$ • www.standardhotel.com*

2 Mondrian

The rooms seem an afterthought at New York hotelier Ian Schrager's celebrity outpost. The Cuban-Asian eatery, pool deck, and hip Sky Bar provide stylish hobnobbing territory. ◈ *Map M3 • 8440 Sunset Blvd • 323-650-8999 • $$$$ • www.ianschragerhotels.com*

3 The Standard Hollywood

Shag is back and the pool is cool at this good-value retro hangout on Sunset Strip. Party in the lobby, which morphs into a lounge at night with DJ-spun music. The pool, intriguingly fringed by indigo-blue Astroturf, is also good for loitering. ◈ *Map M3 • 8300 Sunset Blvd • 323-650-9090 • $$ • www.standardhotel.com*

4 The Grafton on Sunset

Standing next to the Mondrian, the Grafton has a more accessible and low-key ambience. The lobby is flanked by the fashionable Balboa Lounge and a steakhouse and leads to the pool. ◈ *Map L3 • 8462 W Sunset Blvd • 323-654-4600 • $$$ • www.graftononsunset.com*

5 Sunset Marquis Hotel & Villas

This ultra-deluxe West Hollywood hideaway is a favorite with rock'n'roll royalty such as U2. The on-site recording studio is a major draw, but so are the luxurious quarters and the Whiskey Bar *(see p61)*. ◈ *Map L3 • 1200 N Alta Loma Rd • 310-657-1333 • $$$ • www.sunsetmarquishotel.com*

6 Elan Hotel Modern

The lobby and lounge at this stylish outpost display the retro-cool look in vogue, while the rooms are done up in calming natural tones. It's close to shopping and dining, but you could also order room service and pick a movie from the video library. ◈ *Map L5 • 8435 Beverly Blvd • 323-658-6663 • Dis. access in one room • $$ • www.elanhotel.com*

7 Maison 140

An intimate B&B in the former villa of silent movie star Lillian Gish, Maison 140 cleverly fuses French and Asian design accents. Every room is different, but all feature patterned wallpaper and European antiques. The seductively lit Bar Noir is great for a nightcap. Excellent value for money, close to Rodeo Drive. ◈ *Map J6 • 140 S Lasky Dr • 310-281-4000 • $$$ • www.maison140.com*

8 Avalon

This cool Beverly Hills hot spot has intimately lit cabanas that fringe the curvaceous pool. Rooms feature George Nelson lamps and Eames-style chairs. And don't forget – Marilyn Monroe once lived here. ◈ *Map K6 • 9400 W Olympic Blvd • 310-277-5221 • $$$ • www.avalonbeverlyhills.com*

9 W Los Angeles

The chic W is full of surprises, such as the "waterfall" entrance steps and the table games in the lobby. Suites are fully wired for connectivity, and the Mojo eatery and lobby bar are weekend hot spots. ◈ *Map C2 • 930 Hilgard Ave • 310-208-8765 • $$$ • www.whotels.com*

10 Viceroy

The couple behind the stylish Maison 140 and Avalon has created a fantasy environment that transports guests back in time to Colonial England. The decor mixes kitsch and sophistication, with a grown-up color palette of grey, bright green, and soothing cream. ◈ *Map A4 • 1819 Ocean Ave • 310-260-7500 • $$$ • www.viceroysantamonica.com*

Left & Right **Hollywood Celebrity Hotel**

TOP10 Budget Hotels & Hostels

1 Stillwell Hotel

One of the best bargains in downtown, the Stillwell puts you within walking distance of the Staples Center. It's in a well restored early 20th-century building and has a popular Indian restaurant and a graceful old-time cocktail lounge. ✆ *Map T5 • 838 S Grand Ave • 213-627-1151 • $ • www.stillwell-la.com*

2 Hollywood Celebrity Hotel

Despite the name, celebrity encounters are exceedingly unlikely in this budget gem, a stone's throw away from Hollywood and Highland. But the inviting burgundy awning and Art Deco lobby lead to nicely sized rooms with walls with cartoonlike murals. Rates include a small breakfast as well as parking. ✆ *Map P2 • 1775 Orchid Ave • 323-850-6464 • $ • www.hotelcelebrity.com*

3 Hollywood Orchid Suites Hotel

An excellent base of operation for those wanting plenty of space. Some suites are like small apartments with full kitchen, living room, and bedroom. The decor is a bit long in the tooth, but it's all well kept. With a pool and rooftop sundeck for perks, this place offers good value, indeed. ✆ *Map P2 • 1753 Orchid Ave • 323-874-9678 • $ • www.orchidsuites.com*

4 USA Hostel

Those traveling on a tight budget will find this friendly Hollywood hostel a good jumping-off place for their explorations. Rates include hot beverages, pancake breakfast, linen, and lockers. The lounge has a view of the Hollywood Sign. ✆ *Map Q2 • 1624 Schrader Blvd • 323-462-3777 • $ • www.usahostels.com*

5 Beverly Laurel Motor Hotel

This 1950s-style motel with a small pool is within walking distance of the Farmers Market, Melrose Avenue, and the Beverly Center. Framed art and cheerful bedspreads adorn the rooms. The downstairs diner, Swingers, is popular *(see p109)*. ✆ *Map M4 • 8018 Beverly Blvd • 323-651-2441 • No dis. access • $*

6 Beverly Hills Reeves Hotel

A B&B that doesn't offer much in terms of amenities or style, but you can truthfully brag that you have stayed in Beverly Hills. Converted from an apartment building, it's a short walk away from the goodies of Rodeo Drive. ✆ *Map K6 • 120 S Reeves Dr • 310-271-3006 • $*

7 Farmer's Daughter Hotel

The "price is right" at this motel opposite the Original Farmers Market and CBS, which explains its popularity with game show contestants taping at the TV studio. The staff is willing to organize tickets if you'd like to be part of the audience. ✆ *Map M5 • 115 S Fairfax Ave • 323-937-3930 • $ • www.farmersdaughterhotel.com*

8 Sea Shore Motel

A Santa Monica budget abode, it is perfect for those who favor location over luxury. Only two blocks from the beach, it is on trendy Main Street with wonderful shopping and dining. ✆ *Map A5 • 2637 Main St • 310-392-2787 • No air conditioning • $ • www.seashoremotel.com*

9 Inn at Venice Beach

The beach beckons outside this small hotel on the border of Venice and Marina del Rey. Rooms offer moderate comforts and a cheerful decor. Rates include breakfast. ✆ *Map A6 • 327 Washington Blvd • 310-821-2557 • No dis. access • $$ • www.innatvenicebeach.com*

10 Safari Inn

Easily recognized by its classic neon sign, this retro motel has undergone a facelift. Rooms, some with full kitchens, now sparkle in peach and blue. Close to Universal, NBC, and Warner Bros studios. ✆ *Map E3 • 1911 W Olive Ave • 818-845-8586 • $ • www.coasthotels.com*

Unless otherwise stated, all hotels accept credit cards, have private bathrooms and air conditioning, and provide disabled access

Price Categories

For the cheapest standard double room per night (without breakfast), taxes, and extra charges.	$ under $100
	$$ $100–$150
	$$$ $150–$250
	$$$$ $250–$350
	$$$$$ over $350

Loews Santa Monica Beach Hotel

🔟 Family Hotels & Motels

1 Wyndham Bel Age Hotel

Close to Sunset Strip, this old but upscale property has balconied suites and excellent views, truly breathtaking from the rooftop pool and Jacuzzi. Children under 18 stay free with parents. ✪ Map L3 • 1020 San Vicente Blvd • 310-854-1111 • $$$ • www.wyndham.com

2 Magic Castle Hotel

Pennywise travelers love this hotel close to Hollywood action. Units vary in size but full kitchens help cut down on restaurant bills. Guests also enjoy access privileges to the Magic Club in a nearby mansion. ✪ Map P2 • 7025 Franklin Ave • 323-851-0800 • No dis. access • $ • www.magiccastlehotel.com

3 Best Western Hollywood Hills

Other hotels may have more stylish rooms, but the ones at this central Hollywood property offer plenty of elbow space and recently redone baths. The tiled pool and coffee shop are welcome assets. ✪ Map Q2 • 6141 Franklin Ave • 323-464-5181 • $$ • www.bestwestern.com/hollywoodhillshotel

4 Sheraton Universal Hotel

Although this property can't shake off the institutional feel of a chain hotel, its location next to Universal Studios is a bonus. Free shuttles to Universal. ✪ Map D2 • 333 Universal Hollywood Dr • 818-980-1212 • $$ • www.sheraton.com

5 Doubletree Westwood Hotel

Located in Westwood village, this family hotel allows you easy access to lots of shops, restaurants, and theaters. It includes a full-service restaurant, bar, swimming pool, gym, and gift shop. ✪ Map C2 • 10740 Wilshire Blvd • 310-475-8711 • $$$ • www.doubletreelawestwood.com

6 Century Wilshire Hotel & Suites

Steps from Westwood's shops and eateries, this well-run hotel has an old-fashioned feel and a multilingual staff. Days start with complimentary breakfast and could end with a relaxing dip in the pool with a kid-friendly shallow end. ✪ Map C2 • 10776 Wilshire Blvd • 310-474-4506 • Dis. access in one room • $$ • www.centurywilshirehotel.com

7 Cal Mar Hotel Suites

The flowery bedspreads and sofas may be stuck in the 1980s, but you get an entire apartment for less money than a standard double anywhere else. Units face a landscaped pool. Located in a quiet residential street, Cal Mar is close to Santa Monica hip zones. Free parking. ✪ Map A3 • 220 California Ave • 310-395-5555 • No dis. access • No air conditioning • $$ • www.calmarhotel.com

8 Loews Santa Monica Beach Hotel

Very close to the sand and Santa Monica Pier, this large resort makes children feel comfortable with activities, special welcome kits, and free stays for those under 18. ✪ Map A4 • 1700 Ocean Ave • 310-458-6700 • $$$ • www.loewshotels.com

9 Disney's Grand Californian Hotel

The price tag is a bit steep at this 751-room resort designed in richly wooded Craftsman style, but standard rooms sleep up to two adults and four kids, and there's even a private entrance to Disney's California Adventure. ✪ Map G5 • 1600 S Disneyland Dr • 714-956-6425 • $$$$ • www.disneyland.com

10 Portofino Inn & Suites

This brand-new, all-suite hotel is great for wallet-watchers. The little ones will love camping out in bunk beds and a sofa sleeper and will get their own amenities such as TV, microwave, and fridge as well. ✪ Map D3 • 1831 S Harbor Blvd • 714-782-7600 • $ • www.portofinoinnanaheim.com

Left **Hilton Checkers Hotel** Center & Right **Renaissance Hollywood Hotel**

TOP 10 Business Hotels

1 Westin Bonaventure Hotel

With about 20 eateries, pool, fitness club, shops, and a full business center, the landmark Bonaventure has more facilities than most small towns. Regular rooms are smallish, but the office suites are well equipped. ◈ Map U4 • 404 S Figueroa St • 213-624-1000 • $$$ • www.westin.com

2 Hilton Checkers Hotel

An island of old-world sophistication in the fast-paced Financial District, this 1927 hotel is great for conducting business in style. Prepare for your meetings in lovely leather chairs at a marble desk. ◈ Map U5 • 535 S Grand Ave • 213-624-0000 • $$$ • www.hilton.com

3 Omni Los Angeles Hotel at California Plaza

Walk to Walt Disney Concert Hall, MOCA, and other downtown landmarks from this modern hotel in the Financial District. Business rooms have huge desks, office equipment, and supplies. ◈ Map V4 • 251 S Olive St • 213-617-3300 • $$$ • www.omnihotels.com

4 New Otani Hotel & Garden

This Little Tokyo hotel offers an exotic experience, especially if staying in the Japanese rooms where you sleep on *tatami* mats. The spa and the beautiful third-floor Japanese gardens are great for winding down. ◈ Map W4 • 120 S Los Angeles St • 213-629-1200 • $$ • www.newotani.com

5 Renaissance Hollywood Hotel

Managed by Marriott, this art-filled high-rise overlooks Hollywood and Highland. Suites accommodate small meetings. An equipped business center, PC rentals, and secretarial services are also on offer. ◈ Map P2 • 1755 N Highland Ave • 323-856-1200 • $$$ • www.renaissancehollywood.com

6 Orlando Hotel

Suitable for smaller gatherings, the trump card of this European-style hotel is its location close to the shopping and nightlife in West Hollywood and Beverly Hills. Rates include a daily taxi voucher. ◈ Map M5 • 8384 W 3rd St • 323-658-6600 • $$ • www.theorlando.com

7 Le Meridien Hotel at Beverly Hills

Friendly and efficient staff, a business center with high-speed Internet access, and meeting rooms with assets such as teleconferencing and video equipment are just some of the great perks. ◈ Map L5 • 465 S La Cienega Blvd • 310-247-0400 • $$ • www.lemeridien.com

8 Luxe Hotel Sunset Boulevard

A lovely property with lush landscaping, this is conveniently located right next to Freeway 405. Spacious rooms in soothing colors feature extras such as DSL and fax machines. ◈ Map C2 • 11461 Sunset Blvd • 310-476-6571 • $$ • www.luxehotels.com

9 Century Plaza Hotel & Spa

This hotel next to Beverly Hills hosts major events, from political fundraisers to pharmaceutical conferences. An overhaul spruced up the pool area and the rooms and added an Asian-inspired spa. ◈ Map C2 • 2025 Ave of the Stars • 310-277-2000 • $$$ • www.centuryplazala.com

10 Los Angeles Airport Marriott

Close to LAX, this chain hotel is great for those who just want to get on with serious business. With just over 1,000 rooms, it has a full range of conference facilities with business and secretarial services for business persons. ◈ Map C4 • 5855 W Century Blvd • 310-641-5700 • $$$ • www.marriott.com

 Unless otherwise stated, all hotels accept credit cards, have private bathrooms and air conditioning, and provide disabled access

Price Categories

For the cheapest standard double room per night (without breakfast), taxes, and extra charges.

$	under $100
$$	$100–$150
$$$	$150–$250
$$$$	$250–$350
$$$$$	over $350

Left **Venice Beach House** Right **The Lord Mayor's Inn sign**

1 Venice Beach House

Built in 1911 by relatives of Venice founder Abbot Kinney *(see p118)*, this delightful inn is a witness to Venice history. A quiet oasis, it allows you to retreat to the comforts of cozy, antique-filled rooms after a busy day at the beach or in town. ◈ *Map A6 • 15 30th Ave • 310-823-1966 • $$ • www. venicebeachhouse.com*

2 Lord Mayor's Inn

Rooms in the main house, built in 1904 as the home of a local mayor, offer the typical B&B vintage feel. Adjacent cottages are also charming and fitted with all the modern comforts. ◈ *Map E2 • 435 Cedar Ave • 562-436-0324 • $ • No dis. access • No air conditioning • www. lordmayors.com*

3 Channel Road Inn

A Neo-Colonial home built in 1915, it is clad in wooden shingles and sits on the northern edge of Santa Monica. Each room has different perks such as fireplaces, lovely four-poster beds, patios, soaking tubs, or a view. ◈ *Map B3 • 219 W Channel Rd • 310-459-1920 • $$$ • www. channelroadinn.com*

4 Artists' Inn & Cottage

An early 20th-century beauty, this inn backs up against a rose garden and has ten rooms with designs that are inspired by Van Gogh, Gauguin, and other artists or artistic periods. ◈ *Map D2 • 1038 Magnolia St • 626-799-5668 • $$ • www.artistsinns.com*

5 Bissell House

This stately 1887 Victorian home has a prestigious address on Pasadena's "Millionaire's Row." A sedate, grown-up atmosphere reigns in the elegant public areas and all the eight cosy guest rooms. ◈ *Map F2 • 201 Orange Grove Ave • 626-441-3535 • No dis. access • $$ • www. bissellhouse.com*

6 The Secret Garden

Just steps from Sunset Strip, each of the five rooms of this Spanish-Mediterranean home is unique. The hosts whip up amazing breakfasts. ◈ *Map M2 • 8039 Selma Ave • 323-656-3888 • Dis. access in one room • Air conditioning is limited • $ • www. secretgardenbnb.com*

7 Inn at Playa del Rey

A modern breezy B&B, close to the ocean and adjacent to a nature preserve, it is perfect for those who want the convenience of staying near the airport. ◈ *Map C4 • 435 Culver Blvd • 310-574-1920 • $$$ • www. innatplayadelrey.com*

8 Inn on Mt. Ada

Live it up in the grandeur of William Wrigley's former hilltop mansion on Catalina Island. Standard rates include breakfast, a light lunch, evening champagne reception, and the use of a golf car so that you can tool around town. ◈ *398 Wrigley Rd • 310-510-2030 • No dis. access • No air conditioning • $$$$ • www. catalina.com/mtada*

9 Dockside Boat & Bed

A unique getaway, this floating B&B has on offer a fully equipped sailboat, motor yacht, or even a Chinese junk. Boats are moored in Long Beach's Rainbow Harbor; enjoy sunset views of the *Queen Mary*. ◈ *Map E6 • 316 E Shoreline Dr • 562-436-3111 • No dis. access • Limited air conditioning • $$$ • www.boatandbed.com*

10 Sea Mountain Inn

Serenity rules at this exclusive retreat tucked away in the mountains high above Malibu. Unwind with a massage or in your room before a wood-burning fireplace. A range of modern communication devices makes sure that you don't lose touch with the real world. ◈ *Address only given with reservation • 310-788-0224 • $$$$ • www. theseamountain.com*

All B&Bs include breakfast as part of room charges

General Index

Index

Acknowledgments

The Author
Catherine Gerber has
observed and documented
the evolution of Los
Angeles in word and image
for nearly 20 years. She
remains fascinated by her
adopted home's ability
to continuously and
unapologetically reinvent
itself. Her work has
appeared in books, news-
papers, and magazines
in USA and Europe.

Photographer
David Peevers

Additional Photography
Max Alexander, Steve
Gorton, Dave King,
Susanna Price, Neil
Setchfield

AT DK INDIA:
Managing Editor
Aruna Ghose

Art Editor
Benu Joshi

Project Editor
Kajori Aikat

Project Designer
Priyanka Thakur

Senior Cartographer
Uma Bhattacharya

Cartographer
Suresh Kumar

Picture Researcher
Taiyaba Khatoon

Fact Checker
Janet Grey

Indexer & Proofreader
Bhavna Sharma

DTP Co-ordinator
Shailesh Sharma

DTP Designer
Vinod Harish

AT DK LONDON:
Publisher Douglas Amrine

Publishing Manager
Jane Ewart

Revisions Co-ordinator
Mani Ramaswamy

Senior Cartographic Editor
Casper Morris

Senior DTP Designer
Jason Little

DK Picture Library
Brigitte Arora, Ellen Root

Production Shane Higgins

Picture Credits
t-top, tl-top left, tlc-top left
center, tc-top center, tr-top
right, cla-center left above,
ca- center above, cra-
center right above, cl-
center left, c- center, cr-
center right, clb- center left
below, cb-center below,
crb-center right below, bl-
bottom left, b-bottom, bc-
bottom center, bcl-bottom
center left, br-bottom right.

Every effort has been made
to trace the copyright
holders, and we apologize
in advance for any uninten-
tional omissions. We would
be pleased to insert the
appropriate acknowledg-
ments in any subsequent
edition of this publication.

This Book makes reference
to various Disney copyright-
ed characters, trademarks,
marks, and registered
marks owned by The Walt
Disney Company and

Disney Enterprises, Inc.
The publishers would like
to thank Disney Enterprises
Inc. for their kind
permission to reproduce
the photographs: 7clb,
30cla, 30-31c, 30bc, 31bl,
32tl, 32b, 33t, 34t, 34br,
35cl, 35b and Petersen
Automotive Museum: 102tr

The publishers would also
like to thank the following
individuals, companies, and
picture libraries for their
kind permission to repro-
duce their photographs.

ACESTOCK LTD., London:
Steve Goddard 56bc, 97tr

CORBIS: 3tl, 136tl, 142tr;
Hal Beral 36crb; Yann
Arthus-Bertrand 7crb, 28-
29c, 102cl; Bettmann 35cl,
35b, 38tl, 139t; Kevin Burke
120-121; Dean Conger 30-
31c, 30bc; Steve Crise 62tl;
Richard Cummins 7clb,
19bl, 32tr; Macduff Everton
32b, 33t, 34t; Robert
Holmes 30cla, 39r; Dave G.
Houser 94 cr; Dewitt Jones
28br; Robert Landau 6cla,
22ca, 22br, 34br, 65tr, 86tl,
92tl, 98-99; Richard T.
Nowitz 57tr; Roger
Ressmeyer 127t; Bill Ross
1c; Joseph Sohm;
ChromoSohm Inc. 68-69;
Douglas Slone 6clb; Frank
Trapper 59tr; Peter Turnley
38tr; Nik Wheeler 8cb, 32tl,
113tl, 132-133, 135tl; Alison
Wright 31bl; CORBIS SABA:
David Butow 100tl; CORBIS
SYGMA: Koester Axel 96b.

© J PAUL GETTY TRUST:
Irises by Vincent van Gogh,
Dutch, Saint-Rémy, France,
1889 Oil on Canvas 28 x

Acknowledgments

36-5/8 in. 90.PA.20 12-13c, *Wheatstacks, Snow Effect Morning* by Claude Monet, French, Giverny, 1891 Oil on Canvas 25-1/2 x 39-1/4 in. 95.PA.63 12br, *Venus and Adonis* by Titian and workshop, Italian, about 1555-1560 Oil on Canvas 63 x 77-3/8 in. 92.PA.42 13tl, *Cabinet on Stand* Attributed to André-Charles Boulle, ébéniste; and Jean Varin, medalist, French, Paris, about 1678-1680 H: 7ft. 6-1/2 in.; W: 4ft. 11-1/2 in.; D: 2ft. 2-1/4 in. 77.DA.1, *Abduction by Europa* by Rembrandt Harmensz. van Rijn, Dutch, 1632 Oil on Panel 24-1/2 x 30-5/16 in. 95.PB.7; GRANGER COLLECTION, NEW YORK: 38bl.

© THE HUNTINGTON LIBRARY, ART COLLECTIONS, & BOTANICAL GARDENS: 7tr, 22-23c, 23tl, 23clb, 24tl, 24tc, 24tr, 24bc; INDEX STOCK IMAGERY: Mick Roessler 74–75; LA CONVENTION & VISITORS' BUREAU: Michele & Tom Grimme 137tr

© 2003 MUSEUM ASSOCIATES/Los Angeles County Museum of Art: *La Trahison des Images (Ceci n'est pas une pipe)* by René Magritte, purchased with funds provided by the Mr. and Mrs. William Preston Harrison Collection 16cla, *Mother about to Wash Her Sleepy Child* by Mary Cassatt, 1880 Oil on canvas, Mrs. Fred Hathaway Bixby Bequest 16cb, *In the Woods at Giverny: Blanch Hoschedé at Her Easel with Suzanne Hoschedé* by Claude Monet,1887 Oil on canvas, Mr. and Mrs. George Gard De Sylva Collection 17tr, *Flower Day* by Diego Rivera, 1925 Oil on canvas, Los Angeles County Fund 17bl, *Untitled Improvisation III* by Vasily Kandinsky, 1914, Oil on cardboard, Museum acquisition by exchange from David E. Bright Bequest 18tc, *The Magdalen with the Smoking Flame* by Georges de La Tour, c. 1638-40, Oil on canvas, gift of The Ahmanson Foundation 18tr, *Standing Warrior*, West El Arenal Brown style, Mexico, Jalisco, c. 200 B.C. – A.D. 400, Ceramic with burnished red slip and painted black and cream decoration, The Proctor Stafford Collection, purchased with funds provided by Mr. and Mrs. Allan C. Balch MASTERFILE: Gail Mooney 4–5

© 2003 THE NORTON SIMON FOUNDATION: *Still Life with Lemons, Oranges and a Rose* by Francisco de Zurbarán, Spanish, 1633, Oil on canvas 24-1/2 x 43-1/8 in. F.1972.06.P 42tr, *Self-Portrait* by Rembrandt van Rijn, c.1636-38, Dutch, Oil on panel 24-7/8 x 19-3/4 in. F.1969.18.P 90tc, *Exotic Landscape* by Henri Rousseau, French,1910, Oil on canvas 51-1/4 x 64 in. F.1971.3.P 90tr

© RENAISSANCE HOLLYWOOD HOTEL: 150tc, 150tr

© UNIVERSAL STUDIOS HOLLYWOOD: Shrek 4-D 26tr

© 2003 UNIVERSAL STUDIOS INC.: 7cra, 28tr, 26-27c, 27tl, 27bla, 27bc

All other images are © Dorling Kindersley. For further information see *www.dkimages.com*.

Special Editions of DK Travel Guides

DK Travel Guides can be purchased in bulk quantities at discounted prices for use in promotions or as premiums. We are also able to offer special editions and personalized jackets, corporate imprints, and excerpts from all of our books, tailored specifically to meet your own needs.

To find out more, please contact:

(in the United States) **SpecialSales@dk.com**

(in the UK) **Sarah.Burgess@dk.com**

(in Canada) DK Special Sales at **general@tourmaline.ca**

(in Australia) **business.development @pearson.com.au**